❀ ❀ ❀ ❀ ❀

The Political Process

Executive Bureau–Legislative Committee Relations

[REVISED EDITION]

J. LEIPER FREEMAN

Vanderbilt University

RANDOM HOUSE • NEW YORK

134432

The Political Process:

Executive Bureau–Legislative
Committee Relations

STUDIES IN
POLITICAL
SCIENCE

For John, Suzie, Meg, Peter and Polly

Preface to the Revised Edition

This is a modest attempt to make a bit more up-to-date a study published a decade ago. The first edition was the result of a doctoral dissertation written as a student of Professor George A. Graham at Princeton University and also of work as his assistant on the task force on Indian affairs of the first Hoover Commission. Moreover, a great deal of encouragement and guidance was received from Professor Richard C. Snyder, first editor of this Study series. Other colleagues have participated in the author's education over the years, and to them he would like to extend his gratitude while in no way implying their responsibility for his shortcomings.

While teaching at Allegheny College from 1961 to 1964, the author enjoyed the association of many fine undergraduate majors in political science. One of these, David Wion, was an assistant who helped in some of the library work for the revision of the first edition; moreover, he was an inspiration to a professor writing for college generations of the 1960's. I would also like to acknowledge my great gratitude to Mrs. Pauline Mooney who did an excellent job of preparing the final manuscript.

J. Leiper Freeman

Contents

CHAPTER ONE *Analyzing Federal Legislative–Executive Relations*   3

THE AIMS AND UTILITY OF THIS STUDY   5

THE PLACE OF THIS STUDY IN POLITICAL SCIENCE   8

SOME DEFINITIONS   11

CHAPTER TWO *The Setting and the Participants in Bureau–Committee Relations*   13

THE PARTIES, THE ADMINISTRATION, AND CONGRESS AS A POLICY-MAKING SYSTEM   15

    Party Government in the Administration and Congress   17

    The Limitations of Party Government   21

SEMI-AUTONOMY OF SUB-UNITS IN THE POLITICAL SETTING   22

    Semi-Autonomy of Bureaus in the Administration   23

    Semi-Autonomy of Committees in Congress   24

    Semi-Autonomy of Interest Groups in Relation to the Parties   27

CHARACTERISTICS OF SUBSYSTEM LEADERS   28

SUMMARY   31

CHAPTER THREE *Major Influences of the General Political Setting on the Subsystem*   32

INFLUENCE OF THE PRESIDENT AND THE ADMINISTRATION ON THE SUBSYSTEM   33

    Hierarchical Control   35

Informal Influence on Subsystem Actors 40
Restrictions upon Presidential Intervention 42
Assessment of Presidential Influence on Sub-
systems 43
INFLUENCE OF CONGRESS ON THE SUBSYSTEM 46
Differences between House and Senate Mem-
bers' Autonomy 47
Control through Legislative Reorganization 48
Limitations of Discipline and of Joint Action 50
Assessment of Importance of Committee
Members' Roles 54
INFLUENCE OF THE PARTIES ON THE SUBSYSTEM 55
Group Interdiction of Partisan Policy-Making 57
Possibilities of Party Influence 59
SUMMARY 62

CHAPTER FOUR *Relationships Within the
Subsystem: Part One* 66
STRATEGIES AND INFLUENCE OF BUREAU PERSON-
NEL IN THE SUBSYSTEM 69
Using Top-Level Support 70
Legislative Liaison 76
Interpersonal Influence 78
Choosing Alternative Committees 80
Exploiting Committee Hearings 81
The Use of Publicity 84

CHAPTER FIVE *Relationships Within the
Subsystem: Part Two* 88
INTERACTIONS BETWEEN BUREAU LEADERS AND
GROUPS 88
Relations between Bureau Leaders and Non-
Internal Groups 91
Involvement of Groups in Policy Determina-
tion by Bureau Leaders 94

STRATEGIES AND INFLUENCE OF COMMITTEE PER-
SONNEL IN THE SUBSYSTEM   96

Shaping Bureaucratic Application of Laws   96
Behavior and Influence of Substantive Com-
mittee Participants   98
Behavior and Influence of Appropriations
Committee Participants   101
Behavior and Influence of Investigating Com-
mittee Participants   103
Some Contrasting Examples of Investigating
Committee Structures and Effects   106
Committee Staff Influence   111

SOME BASIC FACTORS IN COMMITTEE MEMBERS'
RECEPTIVITY TO POLICY VIEWPOINTS   112

THE EBB AND FLOW OF GROUP EFFECTIVENESS IN
THE SUBSYSTEM   115

CHAPTER SIX *The Subsystem in Perspective*   119

A SUMMARY JUSTIFICATION OF THE STUDY'S FOCUS   119

SOME PROPOSITIONS ABOUT THE SUBSYSTEM   121

Summary Propositions regarding the Bureau
Leaders in the Subsystem   121
Summary Propositions regarding Committee
Participants in the Subsystem   126

NOTES TO THE STUDY   131

INDEX   143

The Political Process:

Executive Bureau–Legislative Committee Relations

CHAPTER ONE

Analyzing Federal Legislative–Executive Relations

The process of policy-making in the leviathan of American national government is a source of anxiety and frustration to many in our society. A few years ago, the late Professor V. O. Key, Jr. received a telephone call from the provoked father of a student in "Gov I" at Harvard. "Sir," said the angered parent, "my son reported to me that one of your lecturers said today that the United States government has elements of *socialism* and always has had some of these elements. He gave as an example our postal system. What is the meaning of this?" Professor Key replied in his calm bass drawl, "Well, I wouldn't worry too much about that if I were you. Judging by the rate of the mail delivery these days, it must be *creeping* socialism."

Charges of socialism, whether creeping or galloping; warnings of mammoth conspiracies; and fears of sinister "complexes" composed of industrial and military groups —all are perennial manifestations of reaction to the growth of positive federal government. This government has had to meet the demands for expanded social services and international commitments in the present world. Its growth has entailed creation and maintenance of a civil bureaucracy and a military establishment adequate to the tasks. Also, its legislative and executive branches have become basically the heart of the positive federal governmental process. At present, its judicial branch is inclined to devote itself more to the correction of constitutional wrongs in the states and less to reviewing the authority of the President and Congress. Such a role for the judiciary only enhances the fears of the modern anti-Federalists. Nevertheless, in the relations of the federal executive and legislative branches to each other and to their political environment lies the general arena in which many of the most crucial public decisions of our day are being made.

Yet to concentrate only upon the very general system of Congress, the Administration, and the political parties tends to obscure crucial features of diversity in the leviathan, leaving one with the picture of an overwhelming concentration of power. In order to understand how issues are resolved and national policies are made, one must view the system as something other than a well-geared monolith. There may even be some consolation for the agonized critics in doing so. Historically, although the federal government has accumulated great power and reached huge proportions in the course of the nation's development, it has done so relatively slowly and usually against considerable resistance from various special interests. Many groups directly or indirectly urge specific expansions of power favorable to themselves but oppose either general expansions or increases of authority specifically favoring other groups. Furthermore, increases in federal power have usually been realized only after limitations imposed by the federal system, by the separation of powers, and by checks and balances have been reasonably satisfied. Perhaps the most significant point, in the last analysis, is that the growth of the federal government has most frequently occurred when new activities have been urged on Congress and the Administration by special segments of the population. If there is any creeping socialism in American government, it has come and is coming largely as an accompaniment of what might be called "creeping pluralism," that is, the gradual growth of political groups especially concerned with the protection and promotion of particular interests. The kind of government which has evolved is far from being a tightly knit leviathan.

THE AIMS AND UTILITY OF THIS STUDY

The present study endeavors to focus attention upon and to state some propositions about the interactions of certain key participants in this pluralistic leviathan. The actors are members of political subsystems centering upon executive bureaus and legislative committees. The chief value to be derived from the study should be a greater understanding of the patterns of policy-making *within* these subsystems. The major focus, beyond an examination of the relations between the general political setting and the participants in the subsystem, is upon relations among subsystem actors from the bureaucracy, from congressional committees, and from interested segments of the public. The value of studying the patterns of influence within executive–legislative subsystems has been well-stated by Professor Ernest S. Griffith, who called them "whirlpools." Griffith said, in part:

> . . . It is my opinion that ordinarily the relationship among these men—legislators, administrators, lobbyists, scholars—who are interested in a common problem is a much more real relationship than the relationship between congressmen generally or between administrators generally. In other words, he who would understand the prevailing pattern of our present governmental behavior, instead of studying the formal institutions or even generalizations in the relationships between these institutions or organs, important though all these are, may possibly obtain a better picture of the way things really happen if he would study these "whirlpools" of special social interest and problems.[1]

In a recent most valuable book, Douglass Cater has similarly analyzed power in Washington in terms of "sub-governments" which are essentially the same as the whirlpools depicted by Griffith.[2] These phenomena are neither new, surprising, nor devious. Rather they are so numerous and increasingly specialized that the mass of the citizenry has difficulty in following them. And as Cater points out, no part of the national political framework can effectively control all of them.

Similarly, a closely related additional value of the study may be a better understanding of the plural patterns of power and decision-making within the national government as they mirror the functional specialization and diversity of American society. This diversity of interests—of groups concerned with special values—has a host of sources deeply rooted in the nation's experience. Geographic dispersion, cultural heritage, religious belief, economic status, technological specialization, and traditions of individual and group self-seeking are but an important few of these sources. The groups arising from them have demanded the attention of special units of Congress and of the Administration and have thereby contributed to the diversity and complexity of the federal government while simultaneously attaining protection from it and niches for themselves within it. At the same time, Congress and the Administration, organized under legal norms which encourage permissiveness and particularism through their many sub-units, have tended to accommodate these interests. Furthermore, they have tended to encourage, aid, and abet their political activity and their very survival. The leaders from the official sub-units have become involved in relationships with leaders of the interest groups and have tended to take over major decision-making functions officially allotted to the government as a whole. By observing how and under what conditions specialists in certain areas of public policy are important determinants of that policy for the overall political system, one may sharpen his understanding of the importance of bureau-committee subsystems in the larger legislative–executive political setting.

Hence, another goal of this study, albeit somewhat secondary, is to depict the salient relationships between the general political setting on the one hand and the actions of members of bureau-committee subsystems on the other. This involves observations of the limitations upon the autonomy of subsystem participants imposed by institutions and individuals in the larger setting. We will also explore the factors contributing to their autonomy and some of the complexities which result.[3]

THE PLACE OF THIS STUDY IN
POLITICAL SCIENCE

The present study is related to a general concern with group politics and political behavior strongly reflected in this generation's literature of political science. Arthur Bentley wrote the pioneering work in the field in 1908.[4] In the same year, Graham Wallas produced a classical study which has served as a foundation piece in political behavior.[5] The frames of reference projected by these men were not utilized extensively for more than a generation; however, the efforts of Pendleton Herring and others enkindled a renewed interest in pressure groups and policy-making in the 1930's and 1940's.[6] By mid-century, David Truman built upon these foundations a systematic treatment of group politics in the American governmental process.[7] In his work, group access to the organs of government and the cross-pressuring effects of overlapping group memberships are ably related to the major areas of the federal governmental system. Also, V. O. Key wrote some concise and well-formulated chapters dealing with the politics of governing as well as with administration as politics, which contributed to the general perspective of this study.[8] Avery Leiserson produced a pioneering treatment of administration as group politics.[9] Moreover, texts and studies dealing with the legislative process and with Congress as an institution are both good and abundant. Most of them contribute considerable insight into the functioning of committees and into legislative–executive relationships. Space does not permit citation of all of them here, but most of them owe something to Woodrow Wilson, whose classic written in 1885 preceded by a generation even the work of the early group-process political writers.[10] Some have as their primary objective the understanding of congressional institutions.[11] Others are more intent upon portraying and explaining the behavior of senators and representatives in relation to the world in which they live.[12] In different ways, all of them shed considerable light upon aspects of the behavior of members of Congress and upon Congress as an institution. They are particularly helpful in portraying the relationships between Congress in general and its pluralistic components, between Congress and the Administration, and between Congress and the parties and pressure groups.

The aforementioned works are general in scope and application, and on the whole they are concerned with the political process at a higher level and on a broader scope than is this study. The same may be said of some excellent mid-century works dealing more explicitly with legislative–executive relations, but several of these are especially relevant as background sources for this study.[13] Moreover, they concentrate more upon the problems of congressional control over the bureaucracy than upon bureaucratic influence upon Congress. In this regard, the comprehensive book just completed by Joseph P. Harris is very useful.[14]

While this increased portrayal of the general legislative process and institutional structure has been unfolding, description and analysis of pressure groups and lobbies have proceeded apace. Recent works by Blaisdell, Milbrath, and Zeigler have been notably good additions. Again, these studies as well as others concerned with the Presidency and the Administration in general are, like the congressional studies cited, relevant but broader in scope.[15]

Works which come closer to the breadth and level of the focus of the present study are case studies of particular subsystems or of particular legislative acts. Empirically based, they have led to specific insights and to particular hypotheses about the policy-making process. Since the publication of the first edition of this book, other good monographs have been added to those of Earl Latham, Stephen K. Bailey, and Fred Riggs, cited a decade ago. They constitute examples of possible contributions to systematic views of the policy-making process to be derived from intense studies of passage of specific legislative acts.[16] Similar additions to the group of studies of particular segments of Congress, the Administration, and special parts of the public in restricted areas of policy-making, have also been made.[17] But there still exists an infinite world of such subsystems awaiting the analytical talents of today's political scientists.

In this book, the author attempts to draw upon an intensive study made a number of years ago of a particular subsystem covering an extensive period of time and including the passage of numerous pieces of legislation and various political maneuvers. The book also utilizes other cases such as those cited above. The major aim still is to state systematically the dimensions both of subsystem relationships to the larger political setting and of relationships within the subsystem, using description as economically as possible for purposes of illustrating propositions.

SOME DEFINITIONS

Subsystem, as used here, refers to the pattern of inter-actions of participants, or actors, involved in making de-cisions in a special area of public policy. Furthermore, although there are obviously other types of subsystems, the type which concerns us here is found in an immedi-ate setting formed by an executive bureau and congres-sional committees, with special interest groups intimately attached. In a strict sense, concentration upon this type of subsystem represents analysis at a lower level in the political structure because the participants are drawn into the interaction primarily as a function of their posi-tions as leaders and members of sub-units of the over-all political system.

The *general setting* of the bureau-committee subsys-tem is the overall federal political system of which the features most relevant for our analysis are the major structures for positive political decision—Congress, the Administration, and the parties. To focus on the prob-lems of legislative–executive relations at a high level of analysis, one might study the institutional relations be-tween Congress and the Administration as shaped by the law of the land and by political parties in their gen-eral outlines. On the other hand, one might choose to study the interpersonal relations of the leaders of these institutions on the assumption that the highest-level personalities are the determiners of policy.

The *immediate setting* of the subsystem, as indicated above, is composed of lesser units of the general polit-ical system, and it is out of their primary relationships to these lesser units that subsystem actors derive their roles as members of the subsystem. One might choose to study the organizational relationships among these lesser units as a whole and thereby break down the institutional relationships of the general political system into more meaningful categories.

Policy-making as used here refers primarily to the formulation, adoption, and application of legal courses of action.

CHAPTER TWO

The Setting and the Participants in Bureau–Committee Relations

At the center of the general public policy-making system of the United States are Congress and the Administration. The latter term conveys a plural notion of the political executive of the United States. It connotes an extensive network leading to and symbolized by the President, rather than a highly personalized and individualized one-man show. The Presidency is the core of the Administration, a core in which one man is very important and is burdened almost beyond belief, but in which he is also officially accredited with functions which are the products of numerous influential individuals and many forces beyond his own personality and predilections.

The President and his Administration on the one hand and Congress on the other both reflect and shape the gross dimensions of political sentiment in American society. In the broad sense, they are the symbols for and the objectives of the two major political parties as the latter attempt to organize and control the government. Consequently, they are the two great focal points of positive power in our national political system.

Long-standing norms of our governmental structure, reinforced by a century and three quarters of legal development and interpretation, encourage public activity in policy-making to direct itself toward both these branches of government. Those who are interested in promoting certain political viewpoints find it necessary to press their views upon two organs of government, each with legitimate power. This normative framework is set forth in part by a legal system of separation of powers and checks and balances between Congress and the Administration. However, the traditional negative view of this system is inadequate for portraying the reality of the situation. Even in legal terms alone, the separation is incomplete. To have checks and balances it has been necessary that powers, instead of being completely separated, be shared to some degree so that each branch could defend itself against the other. Thus the executive shares in the legislative power through the veto, through its ability to address and inform the legislative branch, and through the interpretive aspects of the executive function. The legislative shares in the executive power through its ability to grant or withhold authority, man power, and resources necessary to the executive function and to inquire into the operations of the executive branch for purposes of obtaining information pertinent to proposed legislation. The result is a permissive legal framework in which the two branches are ultimately bound together primarily by felt necessity to get decisions made. They can war and stall much more than is possible in a rigid system where legislative and executive agreement is a legal imperative. Nevertheless, since each has authority and power to withhold from the other those things which it needs and desires, there is a concurrent interdependency urging them to seek mutually satisfactory means and ends, to find a common denominator in the face of their tendencies toward stalemate or worse.

When this legal framework is filled out with human political content, the traditional view of separation of powers becomes even more remote. The major question becomes: "How and with what results will the Administration and Congress together decide for the American people on a policy which will meet certain public needs?" Despite the apparent chaos, confusion, and conflict that characterize relations between the Administration and Congress in all but "honeymoon" periods, one should not be blind to this very real interdependence and need for mutual adjustment. It is especially relevant that the legal framework specifically precludes neither conflict nor cooperation, but rather is flexible and permissive. It will allow diverse social and political forces alternate channels of access to policy-making. Yet it does not outlaw legislative–executive agreement so much as it increases the opportunities for interim disagreement and for the slow exploration of alternatives by a diverse society as it seeks consensus.[1]

THE PARTIES, THE ADMINISTRATION, AND CONGRESS AS A POLICY-MAKING SYSTEM

Much has been written in recent years about either the decline or the inadequacies of party government in the United States. Some authors argue that the strength and cohesiveness of the two major parties in the nineteenth century were much greater than they are today. Many of these commentaries also hold that the increasing complexity of issues, the proliferation of special interests, the growth of a large, nonpartisan bureaucracy, and the gradual alteration of regional, social, and economic conditions have contributed to the devaluation of the two major parties as policy-making mechanisms in comparison to special interest groups. Apparently, the major function of parties is the mobilization of votes to win elections.[2]

It has certainly been evident for some time that the two major parties are internally divided into major factions. Many analysts of party and group politics have clearly portrayed the importance and the diversity of state and local elements of the Democratic and Republican parties. The municipal, county, and state organizations, or factions thereof, concentrate especially upon electing congressmen, senators, governors, legislators, mayors, commissioners, and councilmen. They care relatively little for the national committees. They hold blocs of local power which the national parties need; hence, they tend to determine their own "party lines," even though in doing so they may be considerably at variance with other groups flying the same party banner. It is the chief function of each major national party to bring out of this melange of party blocs a candidate who can win the Presidency in the name of the party and can help create a favorable climate of opinion for the candidacies of his party's congressional nominees. Otherwise, the main task of state and local party elements is the election of representatives and senators, and sometimes they carefully divorce themselves from or even undermine the national-party nominees.[3]

Recent elections have witnessed an increasing tendency toward ticket-splitting, both between gubernatorial and presidential candidates and between congressional and presidential candidates. Professor Burns offers the provocative if not entirely new thesis of "four-party" politics in America, involving presidential and congressional versions of the Republican and Democratic parties. Certainly, his review of political history in the United States points up the coalition nature of national politics and the prevailing effects of the separation of powers, federalism, and factions upon the party structures involved in running the government.[4]

The consequences, stated all too simply, are that within each major party a coalition led by one of the larger intraparty factions succeeds every four years in capturing the leadership of the party as well as the presidential nomination. If it succeeds in attaining the Presidency too, this coalition probably finds that it has done so by rallying in support of its candidate most of the major opposing factions within its own party, plus a considerable group of disaffected members of the other major party. Having gained the Presidency, this coalition sets about establishing an Administration calculated to hold a winning combination together until the next presidential contest.

PARTY GOVERNMENT IN THE ADMINISTRATION AND CONGRESS

In the Administration, power and authority are parceled out in a manner conducive to representing the diverse elements which went into the winning coalition, yet contrived to maintain the ascendancy of the core group chiefly responsible for nominating and electing the President. The majority of top-ranking posts in the Administration and the inner circle of advisors to the President will most likely come from this core group. For the sake of maintaining party unity, other important offices in the Administration are likely to be given to the major opposing faction in the President's party. Still other important offices may be granted to leaders from the disaffected element of the opposite party, as was the case when President Franklin Roosevelt deliberately sought and appointed a Western progressive Republican, Harold L. Ickes, as Secretary of the Interior, and when President Dwight Eisenhower appointed a Texas Democrat, Oveta Culp Hobby, as head of the Federal Security Agency (ultimately changed to the Department of Health, Education, and Welfare). President Kennedy showed a similar pattern in his appointments of the Republicans McGeorge Bundy as White House assistant and Robert S. McNamara as Secretary of Defense; both were continued by President Johnson.

It is less customary for supporters of the defeated presidential candidate to be called into the Administration, since unusual and highly favorable conditions seem to be required to make such appointments effective. President Franklin Roosevelt succeeded in getting well-known long-time Republicans to serve in the War and Navy secretaryships during the emergency period of the early 1940's, when defense policies were placed "above party." President Kennedy accomplished something of the same nature by his appointments of Secretary Dillon to the Treasury and Ambassador Lodge to Vietnam. On the other hand, President Eisenhower's naming of

Martin Durkin, a Stevenson Democrat, as Secretary of Labor, seemed to confirm by Durkin's short stay in office the acute perception of the late Senator Robert Taft, who called the appointment "incredible."

In any event, the Administration is organized and operated by a party that is actually a coalition drawn together on a national level for capturing the Presidency under either a Republican or Democratic standard, with relatively tenuous and sometimes ephemeral roots in some of the traditional local and state organizations. On a national, high-level basis this party is apt to represent the closest approximation of an overall public viewpoint. Although the leaders of the defeated national party can occasionally speak strongly through the defeated presidential candidate and his cohorts, they obviously experience difficulty in maintaining this position because they lack an official forum comparable to the Administration. During the four years of an Administration's tenure, competition in speaking for the national point of view is likely to develop between factions of the Administration itself, giving it a type of functional, "two-party" structure internally, even though most members of either faction nominally claim the Administration's label.

On the congressional side, in both houses, there is no necessary congruence between either the nominal majority or the actual majority and the party in control of the Administration. The congressmen and senators, having been elected by state and local organizations, tend to group into majorities and minorities that transect formal party lines. The pro-Administration coalition comes from "both sides of the aisle," as does its counterpart. The formal party lines hold for the organization of the House and Senate—that is, the selection of the officers of the two bodies and the assignment of committee posts—but they frequently split asunder on policy matters.

The resulting informal "party" structure can only be partially understood by observing formal party memberships. In many situations, it is more like a "four-party" system, despite the similarity of distributions in the House and Senate. There tend to be pro-Administration and anti-Administration segments within both the Democratic and Republican parties. For purposes of policymaking, the significant cleavages often are the majority and minority within the Administration and the majority and minority within Congress; furthermore, for these four groups conventional party symbols often tend to become secondary to major social, economic, geographic, and ideological divisions of public sentiment.

Generally, the Adminstration is better organized and equipped to maintain a common front than is the Congress, even though this front may hide considerable divergence of opinion within the executive branch. In any case, the initiative toward so-called party government stems largely from the Administration and depends to a great extent upon the capacity which the dominant faction in the Administration has for eliciting favorable responses from a majority in each house of Congress. It follows that this is rarely achieved exclusively along formal party lines, if it is achieved at all, but rather through congressional coalitions of interests similar to those incorporated in the Administration itself.

THE LIMITATIONS OF PARTY GOVERNMENT

It is little wonder that political analysts, pointing to the reluctance and inability of parties and the government to achieve detailed, integrated programs at the national level, have periodically proposed different reforms, some calculated to tighten the legislative or the executive structure and some to tighten party structure.[5] The inclination and the capacity to move in the directions urged by these different proposals, although they may have been enhanced somewhat in recent years by innovations in national-party organizations, by congressional reorganization, and especially by overhauling the Administration and the Presidency, are still decidedly limited by prevailing social diversity. National programs depend upon high salience of issues as well as definite and widely shared public sentiments on these issues. Furthermore, areas of broad public agreement, where they do exist, tend to become basic assumptions incorporated into the body of beliefs held necessary to the existence of an organized society. As they become widely accepted, they often become somewhat vague, generalized, and unassailable—so fundamental that they tend to be above partisan consideration. In themselves, they do not furnish the basis for many clearly partisan issues, and such subordinate issues as may develop around alternative means to achieve these ends often tend either to cut across party lines or to arouse limited public interest, even though the Administration, Congress, party leaders, and the press can work up quite a froth about them.

Furthermore, many national political decisions which

are not above party are below party or cross party lines. On the one hand, parties may take little cognizance of some issues because they affect so small a segment of the public that little would be gained by taking a position on them. Party statements on such issues are usually left up to special groups and their leaders, both official and nonofficial. On the other hand, parties may be so cross-pressured by some issues that they avoid decisive stands on them, since to do so might alienate a major segment of the party's support. Consequently, the resolution of such problems tends to fall upon official and nonofficial groups and their leaders.

SEMI-AUTONOMY OF SUB-UNITS IN THE POLITICAL SETTING

Thus, except in the case of issues which in modern terminology become "escalated" to the level of compelling national concern, the resolution of most policy questions tends more often to be left to secondary levels of the political setting. Policy-making is often left to essentially subordinate units of the Administration and Congress. Similarly, the parties often leave issue politics to interest groups. In this sense, such sub-units of the political setting, encouraged by diffused power and functional specialization of political expertise, tend to enjoy a relatively wide range of autonomy. Policy tends to be "farmed out." Although this is not complete autonomy, it is significantly more than would be found in a centralized and strongly hierarchic model.

This semi-autonomous status of lesser units in the general system deserves a brief overview because such units furnish the most intimate portion of the setting of the subsystem. It is from their positions as leaders of these specialized organizations that subsystem participants derive their status as policy-makers.

SEMI-AUTONOMY OF BUREAUS IN
THE ADMINISTRATION

First, in the complex and interdependent structure of the Administration the bureau or its equivalent is frequently the unit of continuity and specialization in a given area of policy. To a considerable extent, departments and agencies are assemblages of bureaus. Although much has been done within the last generation to centralize departmental control through reorganization and departmental staff innovations, many departments and agencies are still to a great degree "holding companies" for bureaus. Of course, during the Eisenhower Administration there occurred an extensive expansion of departmental officers—particularly at the level of assistant secretary. The intent here was to give the political administrators at the departmental level a greater control over the career bureaucracy, and to some extent this development may have brought the focus of legislative–executive relations closer to the departmental heads. Yet in the many more specialized policy decisions which must be reached apart from the main political arena the importance of bureau chiefs is still great.

In this situation departmental leaders are essentially the agents of the Administration's party, that is, of the coalition which controls the Presidency. This tends to be their primary orientation. It is their job, for as long as they are in temporary positions of departmental leadership, to attempt to assert the views of the Administration before the array of bureaus in their charge and to gain compliance with these views. At the same time, of course, they must rely upon the bureaus for expertise and special knowledge, and they must often accede to what may appear to them to be "bureaucratic inertia" or "bureaucratic eccentricity." The bureaus, composed wholly or almost wholly of career personnel and possessed of the technology and the capacity to perform the tasks of the agency, are neither easily moved by the party in power nor overly embarrassed at urging their time-tested viewpoints upon "non-career" leaders in the Administration.

The result is a not-too-delicate seesaw between the politics of the Administration's party and the politics of bureaucratic expertise, specialization, and self-preservation, with bureau leaders frequently fulcrums in the balance.[6]

SEMI-AUTONOMY OF COMMITTEES IN CONGRESS

In its own way the Congress is a complex structure of many interdependent and important subdivisions. Although the total sizes of both the Senate and the House of Representatives have remained stable for several decades, both houses have not particularly abated their tendency to maintain committees on special subjects. The number of standing committees was reduced by the LaFollette-Monroney Reorganization Act of 1946, but this proved only a temporary or partial curtailment of some active sub-units. What was once a standing committee may carry on as a semi-independent standing subcommittee under the new organization. The standing committees are supplemented from time to time with select committees investigating special topics. Senior members of both parties gain status and prerogative with the accumulation of years of service on these committees. They also build up a certain special knowledge about and familiarity with the issues, individuals, and groups concerned in the policy matters handled by their committees.

Furthermore, each house of Congress is in itself a legislative body, since all acts have to pass both houses in identical form in order to become law. This means that each house tends to some degree to duplicate the work of the other as well as to maintain duplicating committee structures. In order to iron out differences between the houses on particular bills, conference committees are used on an ad hoc basis. All of these facts essentially add to the complex and pluralistic committee matrix within which so many decisions are reached in a decentralized fashion. The usage of joint committees on a sustained basis has been limited and has been only partially successful. The committees of each house are baronial centers of power, as Cater, along with every other student of Congress, has noted.[7] And, indeed, the two houses are jealous of each other, leading to such events as the recent inter-committee warfare between the two appropriations committees.[8]

The general consensus of students of Congress, moreover, is that seniority linked to committee power serves effectively to curtail party government, except under conditions of unusual skill in leadership probably coupled with unusual pressure from public opinion. The majority party in each house gains the power to fill the posts of leadership both on the committees and for the houses as a whole. Yet the norm of seniority, in and out of committee, generally means that long-time legislators can exert influence and achieve status somewhat independent of party regularity. Although both parties have tried to maintain semiformal devices for general policy leadership, the policy committees have seldom tried to bind the party members in the two houses. They explore problems and attempt to arrive at acceptable stands. In addition, majority leaders, minority leaders, and their aides try to enforce some party coherence, especially upon major items at issue. But the management of legislation typically is a task shared by several leaders in each house, and often entails cooperation which crosses party lines and must invariably satisfy the committee leaders concerned. Not since the days of Speaker Joe Cannon has the House of Representatives had truly centralized leadership. That power was dispersed among committee leaders—especially the Rules Committee leaders—and party elders. Yet the House seems highly organized in comparison with the individualistic Senate, where Majority Leaders such as Lyndon Johnson and clotures on filibusters are rarities indeed. There, the prevailing power is customarily shared by "the Establishment" composed largely of senior committeemen.[9]

Eighty years ago Woodrow Wilson pointed out that the real decisions of Congress were made in standing committees.[10] Over twenty years later he found that "each committee is a miniature House," although he detected a greater central control over that body in the powerful Speaker of that period.[11] Today, the centrally organized control of the House is somewhat weaker than it was in the early 1900's, and neither the House nor the Senate has fundamentally altered the importance of committees. The basic validity of Wilson's view on committees still seems to hold. Thus in Congress there is a seesaw between the politics of the congressional majority leadership and the politics of the committees in which the influence of special interests and seniority are concentrated. Here committee leaders are often fulcrums in the balance.

SEMI-AUTONOMY OF INTEREST GROUPS IN RELATION TO THE PARTIES

The parties should be viewed as general organizations striving to achieve majority support and interested in the broadest consensus possible. In the United States, while there is a difference in the broad concerns of the two major parties, they are more distinct from each other on the basis of the geographical distribution of their support, social characteristics, and traditional voting habits than because of hard and clear ideological contrasts and disciplined pursuits of interests.

Not having to pursue the entire range of concerns confronted in the attempt to man the government and win the next election, the specialized interest groups are relatively free to seek narrowly those things nearest and dearest to their hearts, pocketbooks, and clients. They can appropriate a party's viewpoint or ignore it, according to its relevance to their limited cause. These groups are organized as limited-purpose groups, whether their association is based on occupation, profession, geography, ideology, or any of a number of common grounds of cohesion. They do not usually seek to control the whole machinery of policy-making, but rather to prevent policies from being made which would injure their special interests and to secure other policies favorable to their interests. In the aggregate, however, these groups are often a basic counterforce to party politics, and they do an effective job of seesawing with the parties. Here interest-group leaders are often ful-crums in the balance.[12]

CHARACTERISTICS OF SUBSYSTEM LEADERS

Having reviewed briefly some of the factors which emphasize the semi-autonomy of subdivisions of the Congress, the Administration, and the public with rela-tion to the larger entities, and having observed that these subdivisions furnish the immediate setting of sub-systems of policy-making somewhat isolated unto them-selves, it is now appropriate to examine briefly some characteristics of the major participants in such a sub-system. We will consider bureau leaders, committee leaders, and interest-group leaders in sequence.

Bureau leaders tend to occupy an ambiguous status in the Administration. They may be viewed on a con-tinuum from more partisan to more professional or more technical. Though some are still appointed by the President, others are members of the career service. Almost all of them are expected to be closer to the pro-fessional and technical end of the spectrum than are departmental leaders, and the trend over the last few decades has been to view bureau heads increasingly on the "career" side of public officialdom. Consequently, bureau leaders are increasingly apt to "stay" when de-partment leaders "go." Furthermore, bureau leaders are judged on the basis of special knowledge and technical performance and less on party adherence. Conversely, bureau leaders are expected to adjust to the orientation of the party in power insofar as it is possible for them to do so within the general limits of their professional and technical standards. They are not expected to be so deeply embedded in the bureaucracy that they are either inaccessible or handicaps to departmental leaders or, on occasion, to the President.

At present, the bureau leader is the mid-level entrepreneur of policy in the executive branch. Standing between the partisan position of the core of the Administration and the special knowledge, interests, and skills of his bureau, he is a spokesman for the civil servants and the clientele of his organization. Frequently, he is a quasi-monopolist of vital information. Finally, he is a major agent of continuity in a particular area of public policy.

On the congressional side, committee leaders are in positions somewhat analogous to bureau leaders in the Administration. Due to the method of their election committee leaders, like all senators and representatives, reflect geographic and other special interests to a considerable degree. Moreover, since they owe much of their own status in the legislative hierarchy to seniority, they usually respect the seniority of others on their committees, to a certain extent without regard to party allegiance. Serving together over the years on a committee may even breed real loyalty and mutual good will among senior members. Still further, the senior members of a committee may establish a close and mutual relationship with committee staff members so that something of a small, legislative "bureaucracy" may exist, with characteristics of stability, endurance, and cohesion not unlike those in an executive unit. Consequently, it is not unusual to find on a committee an in-group composed of senior members of both parties plus staff members of long standing or great prestige. Even with a majority-party affiliation, a newcomer may be an outsider for quite a while. The members of the in-group will tend to make the decisions and to mediate between the committee and the legislative body as a whole.

The interest-group leaders who play important parts in a subsystem are spokesmen for and symbols of special sets of values held by segments of the public. Like bureau leaders and committee leaders, they are usually middle-level entrepreneurs of policy. Within their special subject-areas they are usually well-informed and are likely to be heard; outside these areas, however, they are less likely to prevail. They make it their business to maximize the satisfaction which will appear to flow from their efforts to the members of their associations. A concomitant of this function is that they furnish continuous, special attention to and take constant parts in the deliberations between the bureaus and committees handling the policies affecting their groups. These leaders keep uppermost in their minds and activities the nature of their constituencies, which are frequently similar to the clientele or part of the clientele of the bureau concerned, and which may be parts of the constituencies of the committee members. Occasionally, they claim to speak authoritatively for larger segments of the public than they actually do. They may be prone to ignore the fact that their constituents often are either members of, or are sympathetic toward, other groups with perhaps conflicting interests. Nevertheless, there is little in our system of policy-making that aids in the determination of the true extent of the representativeness of interest-group leaders, and they tend to be heard insofar as they are vocal, organized, cohesive, clever, knowledgeable, and persistent.

SUMMARY

The general political system which centers upon Congress and the Administration furnishes the political setting for policy-making subsystems formed by the interactions of the leaders of congressional committees, executive bureaus, and interest groups. This political setting is the scene of the activities of the major political parties as they attempt to organize and control the government. In both the Administration and Congress, however, party government tends to be characterized by factionalism, necessitating coalitions which cross strict party lines and which are also assemblages of divergent interests held together by rather volatile political cement. In such a general system, policy issues are rarely found to be clearly partisan, for the chief, enduring partisan concern is to capture the government.

Consequently, policy issues tend to be consigned to lower levels of Congress and the Administration for specialized consideration and extensive resolution by those units most intimately concerned. Similarly, the parties tend to leave doctrinal and technological fine points to interest groups. Thus, the overall setting promotes considerable autonomy for bureaus, committees, and interest groups, which are the organs forming the most immediate setting of the subsystems under discussion here. It is out of their positions as leaders of these semi-autonomous, specialized organizations that the major participants in subsystems derive status as policy-makers. As mid-level entrepreneurs of policy, they stand between tightly organized functional groups on the one hand and loosely mobilized general political power on the other.

CHAPTER THREE

Major Influences of
the General
Political Setting
on the Subsystem

The purpose of this chapter is to explore the
nature, extent, and limitations of the influence of the
President and other leaders of the Administration, of
the Congress, and of the political parties upon the
activities and relations of major participants in policy-
making subsystems. This, therefore, constitutes an extension and qualification of the autonomy theme out-
lined in the previous chapter. Attention here, however,
will be especially focused upon some key factors in the
political setting which either contribute or fail to contribute to patterns of behavior in the subsystem evi-
dencing some responsiveness to presidential, congressional, or partisan viewpoints.

INFLUENCE OF THE PRESIDENT AND THE ADMINISTRATION ON THE SUBSYSTEM

We live in a presidential system of government. Most present-day political scientists—in fact, most since Woodrow Wilson went through his metamorphosis—have been sympathetic toward the development of presidential leadership. The neo-conservative political analysts who are not so enchanted with this point of view will usually be found, if their Whiggery is scratched very hard, to be longing for a simpler day, a bygone age.[1] Many of us do, from time to time.

But the apparent biases of political scientists toward presidential leadership must be properly viewed, since these biases are not necessarily evil or inappropriate, nor are they ever far away from the most scholarly writings. In fact, working assumptions are working biases, to be taken as premises in order to proceed with the analysis. Most political scientists today take for granted the explosive developments of the Twentieth Century which have led to the complicated burdens placed upon American government. Looking at American political institutions, they find that the one most likely to furnish the necessary leadership to cope with the modern age is the Presidency. The conservatives try to depict this viewpoint as a sinister, or cynical, plot against local and legislative institutions, when it should be more aptly viewed as an acceptance of conditions and goals emanating from the modern era. Richard Neustadt, in the most significant of the recent books on the President, sums the situation up well:

> . . . A striking feature of our recent past has been the transformation into routine practice of the actions we

once treated as exceptional. A President may retain liberty, in Woodrow Wilson's phrase, "to be as big a man as he can." But nowadays he cannot be as small as he might like.[2]

The occurrences of the middle of this century—the cold war and the problems of sharing the productivity of a scientific, industrial, and urban society equitably among the American population and, indeed, among the world—put presidential leadership at a premium. But as Neustadt has noted, what was exceptional in the decade of "Normalcy" of the 1920's has become virtually routine in the 1960's. It has been routinized to a great degree by the creation of a vast bureaucracy to *meet* the demands of the times, *not to subvert* a free society. And the President, more than anyone else, is in a position to shape control over that kind of government.

Some Presidents will accomplish this better than others. But the Presidency, as an institution and a collective body, will have a daily share in the process in a way surpassing the periods of crisis previously known. In his book, Neustadt deals with the President as a grand strategist, not as a tactician and "clerk." The present book does not aspire to such a lofty and noble enterprise; rather it attempts to depict how organizational politics in the modern American leviathan functions. In this process, the Presidency plays a major role and has a general effect upon the everyday politics of the subsystems.

The President and the Administration possess power which can condition the course of decisions in the subsystem, but which varies in its effect according to several critical factors. One of these factors is the hierarchical control which the Presidency has, via the structure of the Administration, over the bureau leaders. A second factor is the tenuous link between the President and the Administration's leaders on the one hand, and congressional leaders on the other—a link which is forged largely out of informal relations built on party, patronage, reciprocal interests, and interpersonal associations. A third and perhaps most crucial factor is the degree to which the President and the top members of the Administration can assert public-opinion leadership, especially leadership of a substantial majority of the public.

HIERARCHICAL CONTROL

The pattern of hierarchical control from the Presidency down to a bureau is crucial because it helps determine to what extent bureau leaders feel constrained to "play on the Administration's team" when the political game gets rough. To the extent that it exists, formally or informally or both, it is perhaps the most direct channel of presidential and administration influence upon the operations of a subsystem. Some of the more formal factors having a positive effect in this regard are budgetary controls, clearance requirements for proposed legislation, staffing controls, departmental supervision and organization, and restraints on certain types of communication from the bureau to groups outside the hierarchy. In a large executive structure such as the federal government, these formal factors are not to be regarded lightly, because legal authority and procedural arrangements of long standing constitute major guideposts in the system. On the other hand, there are also informal sources of executive leadership crucial to the control of a bureau by the Administration. Yet both formal and informal controls in the hierarchy have limits which prevent the hierarchy from constituting a perfect "pyramid of power."

The Bureau of the Budget and the budget review system established thereunder form one of the more effective formal means of fitting a bureau's plans and operations into the Administration's policy. The tendency of leaders of subordinate units to seek maximum goals and resources is considerably checked by a bottom-to-top system of budget requests and review, the final product being incorporated in the annual budget which the President submits to Congress. The departments and bureaus are restricted by the Budgeting and Accounting Act of 1921 from seeking amounts larger than those in the President's budget when they appear before an appropriations committee. Although this is a significant means of central control, there have been numerous instances in which questioning by legislators has served to introduce into the record a bureau's original requests which the Administration had eliminated or curtailed. This device for circumventing the restrictions of budget procedure is fairly easily employed by a bureau leader with friendly committee members and interest groups.

Moreover, the law provides that bureau proposals for or comments on legislation should be cleared with the Bureau of the Budget to determine whether they are "in accord with the program of the President." This has some effect in maintaining hierarchical control, but the law and the procedure are not so strict that they prohibit bureau leaders' suggestions that are not in accord with the program from going to Congress. Furthermore, congressmen do not react uniformly to presidential endorsement or non-endorsement; thus a bureau proposal may have a good chance of success even if it fails to get official blessing from the White House. There are also some indications that presidential policy control has suffered from the caution of Budget Bureau officials in playing policy roles.[3]

The ability to appoint or to dismiss bureau leaders is an obvious source of control by the President or leaders of the Administration, although it is not a uniform one nor is it always as important as may be supposed. Since some "nonpolitical" bureau heads stay in office through many Administrations, they acquire in the process a Gibraltar-like status buttressed by special knowledge, professional ties, and legislative and popular support. J. Edgar Hoover of the Federal Bureau of Investigation is an outstanding example of this type.[4] Considerably different might be the status of a bureau head like the Commissioner of Indian Affairs, who, as a presidential appointee, may feel considerably constrained at least to work in conformity with the Administration, or who may even tend to be an exceptionally strong advocate and devotee of the current policies of the Administration. However, in the case of this latter type of bureau leader it is important to recognize that the President and the department head are usually prone to depend upon this bureau chief to be an entrepreneur in his special area of policy, to develop proposals, and to put them across in a manner that reflects honor and credit upon the Administration without involving them extensively. In such a situation the source of initiative and enterprise in the bureau's area of policy is still likely to lie predominantly with the bureau leaders.

The President and the Administration also can bring a bureau more into line with the hierarchy through the pattern of supervision and organization of the agency or department of which the bureau is a part. Organizational devices are not merely lines and squares on a chart, but are also channels of influence. The flat pyramid representation of the holding-company type of department usually signifies in human and social terms that several semi-autonomous administrative organizations have been grouped together without provision either for extending their boundaries or for providing a mutual exchange of ideas and some common means of decision-making with other units. Increased departmental authority, which may bring bureau matters closer to the top policy-makers, plus stronger departmental staffs and interbureau committees, can bring about a greater top-level influence upon bureau policy. To some extent, this has been accomplished in the reorganizations which have occurred in the last two decades. Particularly, the growing tendency to clear legislative proposals through department officials is significant in this regard. However, the average bureau leader exhibits strong tendencies to maintain his bureau's boundaries in the face of competition both within and outside his own department, with the result that departmental staffs and interbureau committees often tend to build a higher pyramid of departmental influence on the organization chart than is to be found in the actual patterns of operation.

Another kind of formal control over bureau leaders available to the executive hierarchy is the ability to restrict certain types of communications (in addition to budgetary and legislative) from the bureau to Congress or to the public. Administrative agencies and bureaus are prohibited by law from employing publicity experts without specific appropriations for this purpose and from using public funds in any direct or indirect way, unless specifically authorized, to influence congressmen or the course of legislation in Congress.[5] These are not executive, but legislative controls aimed at the bureaucracy; yet, insofar as they are effective at all, they can help the Administration also to keep the more "publicity-happy" bureau leaders in line. Actually, these laws might be viewed predominantly as examples of legal fiction in our government today. They do not abolish bureaucratic lobbying or public relations activities. Their major consequences are that bureaus and agencies must call their public relations staffs information or education units, and administrative "lobbying" is required to conform to certain protocols of liaison, reference work, public reporting, public speaking, and testifying in reply to congressional inquiry. The fiction supported by these laws may make it more awkward for bureau personnel to conduct publicity and legislative operations, but they continue to do so not only because such communications seem necessary from bureaucracy's viewpoint, but because the legislators and public groups expect suggestions and information from the bureaus. In such circumstances it is natural that a certain amount of "information" is given and "reporting" and "liaison" are done with an eye toward creating general and specific reservoirs of good will.[6]

Although leaders of the Administration may not particularly be aided by the above rules in any attempts to control bureau communications, there is the more effective weapon of the executive order in which the authority of the President has been and is used to forbid the conveyance of classified or other information to Congress or to those who may be called unauthorized persons. The precedent for this dates back as far as Jefferson's Administration. It has proved on many occasions an effective device for defining the boundaries of the executive branch, especially in defense against legislative attack and for restraining some subordinate entrepreneurs in the bureaucracy. Presidents Truman and Eisenhower set the pattern for postwar restrictions as both issued executive orders prohibiting the disclosure of security information by employees of the executive branch. This was unsuccessfully but bitterly challenged by legislators of the McCarthy ilk.

INFORMAL INFLUENCE ON SUBSYSTEM ACTORS

The informal channels of executive influence within the administrative hierarchy are similar to the major means of executive influence upon legislative leaders in a policy-making subsystem, except for the likelihood that executive influence will have more effect within the executive branch. Frequently, the President can use what may be called his personal leadership or bargaining power to spur key individuals toward viewpoints and actions favorable to the Administration. This, as Neustadt so well points out, is above and beyond his literal power of command via executive orders.[7] Furthermore, the President has the special advantage within the executive hierarchy of a nucleus of temporary, politically sympathetic persons whom he has chosen primarily to aid him in the task of orienting bureaucratic opinion toward his party's goals. The bureau leader, no matter how functionally and politically autonomous he may feel, is seldom as likely to feel immune to the blandishments of the President and the inner circle of the Administration as is a congressional committee chairman. This is encouraged by the different roads to power and prestige which exist for bureau leaders and committee leaders, and by the ability of the Administration to determine more intimately the day-to-day social environment within which the bureau chief must exist.

President Johnson furnished an example in the age-old tradition of executive influence in the spring of 1964. He "let it be known publicly . . . that he had ordered James J. Saxon [Controller of the Currency] to get in line and stay there." The process of letting it be known came in the indirect form of two letters written to a committee of Congress and to the Secretary of the Treasury setting forth some policy positions which Mr. Saxon had been defying. No direct command to the Controller was apparently involved, but he "got the word."[8]

With regard to members of congressional committees, however, the Administration is often on difficult ground. The President usually has all he can do to exploit the devices of informal leadership in the attempt to keep the top leaders of the Senate and House in the Administration's camp, even when the Administration's party controls both houses. These leaders themselves cannot always guarantee favorable performances by their committees. Presidential popularity is often somewhat unstable, and generally it can most effectively be utilized to secure legislative cooperation early in an

Administration's tenure. This is especially true when the party's majority becomes smaller in mid-term congressional elections and when hopes of patronage have been largely exhausted. Top-level communications, conferences, and social events with committee chairmen can have the effect of maximizing the chances of committee acceptance of presidential policies, but a strong public following and largess to dispense are usually very helpful in making the Administration's communiqués and sociability effective upon committee leaders. This is not to deny the occasional cruciality of interpersonal relations between top leaders of the Administration and leaders of congressional committees, but it is to say that the ability to lead popular sentiment (to affect votes) and to distribute the power, prestige, and resources of government often are more relevant factors in effective presidential intervention in committee affairs.

RESTRICTIONS UPON PRESIDENTIAL INTERVENTION

Presidential appeals to public sentiment and presidential decisions about patronage and governmental largess are not used indiscriminately, lest their value be seriously reduced. This is likely to require that top-level intervention with committee leaders will be avoided or minimized unless the Administration calculates that no contest will develop or that the matter is so salient to the public and so essential to the political future of the Administration that a showdown must be risked. Too frequent presidential intervention can lower the prestige of office and dissipate the reserve of power needed for major policies.

This tendency to limit top-level intervention by the

MARVIN W. HEATH

Administration or by the President personally applies
to relations with interest-group leaders also. What is
basically at stake here is largely the symbolic, universal
appeal of the Presidency. Although Presidents as individuals and as singular political leaders make decisions
and engage in policy discussions with representatives of
most major interests and of many minor ones in the
land, these are often on a limited or "diplomatic" basis.
Since the appeal of the presidential symbol must be
kept as universal as possible in order for it to be of maximum use to the Administration, the most decisive relationships with groups will tend to be developed in lower
levels of the Administration. These issues can often be
resolved without directly involving the President. Then,
if a presidential stand or statement is required, the
Administration can be relatively sure of the degree of
its acceptability to the most interested parts of the
public. In thus gaining ability to face in many political
directions without losing face, the President and his
Administration tend to reduce central control over
policy negotiations and to push them in the direction
of subordinate administrative personnel.

ASSESSMENT OF PRESIDENTIAL INFLUENCE
ON SUBSYSTEMS

In making a final assessment of the relationship between presidential leadership and the course of the
decisions that are made in a given subsystem, several
general points should be borne in mind. One is that a
bureau leader is often the most direct avenue of presidential influence in the subsystem because he has at
least nominal ties with the Administration. A second
point, however, is that bureau leaders vary greatly in

attachment to the executive branch; hence, we find some bureau leaders more likely than others to rise and fall in their dealings with congressional committees and public groups in accordance with the general state of presidential leadership. A third point is that presidential leadership and prestige can itself gain from successful initiative, imagination, and influence on the part of loyal bureau leaders in their subsystems. Presidential leadership is often an "organizational product."

The conditions under which there is likely to be a maximum affinity between the state of general presidential leadership and the state of bureau leadership in a subsystem are when the hierarchical structure maximizes the Administration's control over the bureau heads; when common ideologies and interests form a bond of identification between the Administration and the bureau leaders; and when the President, the department head, and the bureau chief depend upon each other to some degree for support and action. A clear example of this existed in the New Deal days among President Roosevelt, Secretary of the Interior Ickes, and Commissioner of Indian Affairs John Collier. President Roosevelt and Secretary Ickes backed Commissioner Collier to the hilt when the latter was attempting to get the Committees on Indian Affairs to put through the comprehensive Indian Reorganization Act of 1934. Their joint efforts resulted in considerable success, which reflected favor not only upon the Commissioner and the Bureau, but upon the Secretary and the President. The Commissioner in turn spoke out for the Supreme Court reorganization plan in 1937, a matter not too germane to his jurisdiction. When Senator Burton K. Wheeler and others led a successful movement against the plan in the Senate, the President's defeat was accompanied for the Bureau of Indian Affairs and its Commissioner by increased difficulty with the Senate Committee on Indian Affairs, of which Senator Wheeler was a key senior member.[9]

The special investigating subcommittee of the Senate, which had been looking into Indian policy for many years, became a sounding board and a collection agency for all manner of charges against the Bureau and, indirectly, against the New Deal. This amazing legislative group had a life of sixteen years, spanning nearly the entirety of the Hoover and Roosevelt regimes. Its last six years were marked especially by its affinity for charges of communism and corruption in the New Deal for Indians. The Bureau, in confronting these, paid a price for its closeness to the higher echelons.

The obverse of the above case can be found in those situations in which leaders of bureaus or similar units are, more or less, permanently divorced from strong identification with the Administration and permanently wedded to Congress. Among the clearest examples of this type are leaders of the Corps of Engineers of the Army, whose ins and outs with Presidents and with the Bureau of Reclamation have been well-described by Maass in the literature.[10]

Within the limits defined, the President and the Administration tend to have considerable leeway to influence participants in a subsystem—especially bureaucratic participants. Yet to oversimplify the role of the President would be to overlook the tenuous nature of top-to-bottom influence in the executive branch and the area of autonomy of bureau leaders.

INFLUENCE OF CONGRESS ON THE SUBSYSTEM

Just as the Administration has difficulty in holding its subdivisions together in a form that enables it to present to Congress and to the public a coherent presidential program, so does Congress lack a strong inclination and the ability to control its own subdivisions. In fact, the congressional problem is more difficult in several ways. For one thing, there is the matter of two houses, each in itself a legislative branch firmly embedded in the Constitution and without the authority or power to determine which one has the final say. For another, there is the problem of a working theory of representation which would bring emphasis upon the general interest. Responsiveness to geographic, economic, and social divisions is built into the two houses by the nature of the methods of election of their members.[11] As a third major facet of the problem, party organization and direction and debates on the floor are comparatively weak, and seniority and committee autonomy are comparatively strong, a situation which blends with the other factors to make Congress perhaps the largest single problem for those who would have a more universal level of discourse and decision in the federal government. In fact, the hypothesis can be advanced that even the tightest Administrations will tend to break apart toward subsystem decision-making because of the necessity of working with this intricate, centrifugal legislative branch.

DIFFERENCES BETWEEN HOUSE AND SENATE
MEMBERS' AUTONOMY

A slight difference between the two houses is observable in the autonomy of individual members and of committee leaders vis-à-vis the general body. Members of the House of Representatives are more "organized," that is, they tend to have less opportunity for individual self-expression, are more restricted by general House rules, and in general conduct their affairs more formally. This means that debates on the floor of the House are more highly structured and limited; moreover, the Speaker, the Rules Committee, and floor leaders in the House tend to have a greater effect on general discussion than their Senatorial counterparts. But it does not necessarily mean that committee leaders of the House are more autonomous and more influential in relation to the general body than are the committee leaders of the Senate. The committee leaders of the House, as well as its individual members, reflect somewhat the impact of the greater organization and discipline imposed by its general leadership and its rules.

Although the difference in tendency toward autonomy between House committee leaders and Senate committee leaders is in any case mild in degree and not always consistent, much of it seems to flow from the differences in the degree of "rugged individualism" generally found in the two bodies. Two relevant factors here may be the larger number of representatives and the shorter terms of their office. The greater size of the House compels more overall organization. The two-year term of office lessens the average job security of representatives and creates a likelihood of quicker average turnover in membership. The short term of office combines with the size of total membership to allow a smaller percentage of representatives than senators to achieve well-entrenched positions and to stand out as independent spokesmen. What can possibly be added to both of these factors is the assumption that a senator "speaks for more people" than a representative (although this is not the case in a state like Nevada, which has two senators and only one representative), and apparently the corollary assumption is that a senator must be allowed more time to state his case.[12]

CONTROL THROUGH LEGISLATIVE REORGANIZATION

As was pointed out in the preceding chapter, the attempt in both houses to effect greater overall cohesiveness and to reduce the number of committees which could serve as standing sources of centrifugal power has met with only limited success. Reduction in the number of standing committees is partially offset in the long run by re-establishment of abolished committees, by maintenance of standing subcommittees, and by a proliferation of select and investigatory committees. Although the LaFollette-Monroney Reorganization Act of 1946 was a considerable move toward reform and centralization of congressional organization and procedure in view of the many barriers to such a venture, it did not move radically in that direction. It particularly did not move far in the development of the means by which the legislative branch could present a coherent front to the executive, nor did it particularly strengthen the means of overall legislative–executive joint action. Quite apart from the decentralizing steps which have been taken in Congress subsequent and counter to the

LaFollette-Monroney Act, the Act itself tended to produce the following major consequences. First, it moved
legislative decision-making toward a smaller number of
discrete centers, but in the process it left the chairmen
of the new consolidated committees more powerful insofar as their jurisdictions had in fact been enlarged.
Second, it strengthened committee staffs, giving the
new centers of power increased bases of information
independent of the bureaucracy and granting the committee leaders some fairly important sources of patronage. Third, it increased the general research and "intel-
ligence" facilities of the Congress embodied in the
Legislative Reference Service, but left this organization
rather inarticulate with respect to the overall leadership of the two houses. As a reference organization the
Service handles the requests of those who refer to it—
primarily individual legislators, committee leaders, and
committee staff members.[13]

In addition, the Act attempted to control, through
the weight of public opinion, the activities of individuals and groups engaged in influencing legislation by
requiring their registration and the filing of their ex-
penses for the public record. Subsequent investigations
of the effect of this provision have not indicated that
any avalanche of public hostility has poured down upon
the groups which have so registered and filed. Also, in
a number of instances it has appeared that individuals
or groups (perhaps needlessly shy in view of the effect
of the law) have been able to rationalize not register-
ing when suspicion was strong among investigators that
they actually engaged in lobbying.

In the Buchanan Committee investigation of lobbying in 1950 through 1951 one bit of evidence particu-

larly demonstrated the problem of attempting to single out certain interest groups as examples of lobbies which the Congress should "regulate." In this instance, the American Enterprise Association introduced into the Committee's records excerpts of letters from some ninety-three senators and representatives from both political parties, all testifying to the value of the information service which the Association had made available to the Congress. It was difficult for the Committee to write a strong statement against this organization.[14]

Nearly a generation has passed since the enactment of the LaFollette-Monroney legislation. The growing concern for congressional reform has produced many good studies of legislative institutions and behavior. Yet, the tightening of controls and centralizing of responsibility through further major reorganizations seem no more imminent in the 1960's than in previous years. And one is tempted to conclude that, on the whole, the last major reorganization did not substantially alter Congress in its pluralism.

LIMITATIONS OF DISCIPLINE AND OF JOINT ACTION

The skepticism of the leaders and the general membership of Congress about the wisdom of centralized control within the two houses is reflected in their reluctance to discipline individual members. This seems to hold true even in instances in which strong ethical considerations as well as the good name of Congress are at stake. There seems to be a propensity to let either the courts (in cases of demonstrable criminal acts) or the constituents of the offending legislator take care of the matter or to let it blow over, despite the existence of legal means by which the legislative bodies can either censure or expel occasional bad actors in their midst. There often seems to be a charitable closing of congressional ranks in which the average member says, "Some day I might be in a tight spot, and I would want my colleagues to judge me lightly too."

The same comments would apply to disciplining a committee which got out of hand. The Rules Committee conceivably could recommend in either house that the funds supporting the work of a particular committee be cut. However, if a committee is a going concern and if its budget requests are not adjudged "out of line" or unreasonable, this avenue of centralized control is not likely to be exploited. In the controversy over the McCarthy Senate Investigating Subcommittee, Senator Guy Gillette of Iowa stated to the Senate and to the public that curtailing the funds of McCarthy's group was one possible way of controlling the method and scope of its investigations. An astute news reporter pointed out to Senator Gillette that he had not made this attempt himself when he had sat as a member of the Rules Committee a few months earlier and had passed on the various committee budgets, even though the methods and scope of the McCarthy investigations had been under criticism for a long time before that. Senator Gillette replied that he had merely said that this was one way the McCarthy Committee could be controlled, but that he would not ordinarily take such a step himself, nor would the Senate Rules Committee generally do so.[15]

Further evidence of congressional resistance to overall coordinated policy-making is reflected in the limited use of joint committees and the duplication of committee work between the two houses. Of course, joint conference committees are appointed ad hoc to adjust the differences between the Senate and House on bills which each has passed in different form. These committees, however, are set up primarily for major pieces of legislation, and their specific function is to represent the views of both houses in arriving at a compromise. They are not permanent structures.

Other than conference committees, there are relatively few examples of joint organization between the Senate and House, although the number of standing joint committees has increased slightly since 1946. The Atomic Energy Committee is the outstanding example of a continuing, decisive organ of this type.[16] From time to time the suggestion has been made that a joint committee on appropriations be established. Yet, even in this vital area in which the executive branch has done a fairly thorough job of obtaining an overall view through the Bureau of the Budget, Congress has resisted the establishment of a joint committee to consider the budget. The House Appropriations Committee (operating to a great extent through powerful subcommittees) first cuts the budget as far as it dares or even farther perhaps, knowing that the Senate Appropriations Committee (again operating to a great degree through subcommittees) will probably recommend some restorations. In fact, this common pattern has resulted in a standing and well-worn observation in Washington that "the Senate is called the 'upper' house because it is always 'upping' the appropriations voted by the House." A competent study analyzing this pattern in the case of appropriations for the Army, done by the late Elias Huzar, noted this fairly constant difference in perspective between members of the House and Senate Appropriations Committees.[17]

In addition to the budget of the government, the budget of the nation—that is, national economic planning—is another area in which comprehensive action has been possible in Congress but has not materialized. The Joint Committee on the Economic Report acts largely pro forma upon the President's economic message, which is based in turn on the report of the Council of Economic Advisors. The Committee's action does not succeed in binding Congress to an annual comprehensive framework or plan into which it fits specific economic measures.

There have been certain instances in which the Senate and House substantive committees in a given policy field have managed to hold joint hearings, usually when the leading members of the two committees have been able to come to some general agreement as to the necessity for vigorous action. In such cases the joint committees are likely to carry great weight with Congress as a whole, since their combined reports and other evidence of consensus by the standing "experts" of both houses restrict the opportunities for opponents of the committee members' views to introduce their opinions into Congress. Although such joint hearings furnish more concerted action upon policy between the two houses, they do not necessarily reduce the importance of committees in policy-making. On the contrary, they probably enhance the power of the two committees taken together in relation to the whole membership of Congress. A small-scale example of what powerful effects can be produced by joint action of standing committees was furnished in the Eighty-third Congress by the joint hearings and recommendations of the Senate and House Subcommittees on Indian Affairs. The joint proposals of members of these two units for transferring services of the Indian Bureau to other agencies and for transferring responsibility for Indian affairs from the federal government to the states made more of a legislative impact than any similar attempts during the previous two decades, despite some continuing opposition from the Bureau and from many Indian spokesmen.[18]

ASSESSMENT OF IMPORTANCE OF COMMITTEE MEMBERS' ROLES

Apparently the factors discussed here and the whole tradition of Congress combine to encourage the preservation of committee and subcommittee centers of power in which groups and individuals operate with considerable effect upon public policy. Perhaps legislators would rather aim for these posts for themselves than curb or abolish them, even when other conditions favor their curtailment. Hence they play the game according to the long-standing custom of live and let live.

The committees profit from the tremendous pull that Congress, as a symbol of power, exerts upon bureau leaders. Bureaucrats tend to judge that their reputations and their bureaus' reputations "on the Hill" can often make or break them in the long run. Therefore, the legislative branch gets considerable homage directly from them. Individual legislators get preferential treatment when they make requests, and bureau leaders will go to great lengths to cooperate—so much so that they will suffer numerous inconveniences and disturbances of normal policy that might not ordinarily be tolerated.

Due to the specialization of function and interest within Congress and the Administration, those committees which deal frequently with a particular bureau tend to become for that bureau the embodiment of "the Hill." Leaders of those committees obtain unusual access to the bureau's officials and to its business. They become the channels through which images of the bureau's leaders, operations, and needs are projected before the general membership of each house. In cases in which presidential leadership does not seem to be highly related to a bureau leader's influence in a subsystem the chances are that this bureau leader is strongly oriented toward the legislative branch in general and toward certain committees in particular. Consequently, the decentralized structure of Congress allows its committee leaders to challenge the Administration for the primary loyalty of its subordinates.

INFLUENCE OF THE PARTIES ON THE SUBSYSTEM

Parties and party leaders are in positions of interdependence with interest groups and their leaders. The leaders of the parties are, roughly speaking, long on general vote-organizing ability and short on programs and issues that move groups of people with special ideologies. Leaders of interest groups are, in turn, long on programs, issues, and ideologies and short on general vote-organizing ability. A great deal of the party leaders' success stems from capitalizing upon situations in which, at least temporarily, they can adopt programs which will swing large proportions of key interest groups to the support of their candidates. Moreover, leaders of the party in power seek to reward groups which supported them and perhaps to win over others through the distribution of public favors. They may even try to split a group or capitalize upon a split in a group by coopting some of its leadership. Such tactics are conceivable with regard to all of the Big Three—business, labor, and agriculture—since it is possible, within limits, to play small business against big business, or the AFL-CIO against independent unions, or the Farm Bureau against the Farmers Union.

Group leaders in turn want the general support of the party in power to an extent sufficient at least to prevent their security from being threatened and preferably to further their aims. Parties usually have reserves of support of a type which many group leaders cannot easily tap by themselves because their aims and symbols are usually too narrow to appeal to a large audience. In this sense, interest-group leaders need party leaders to help them gain allies.

Although party leaders resist being tabbed with special-interest labels, interest-group leaders probably resist partisan labels even more emphatically. At any rate, even the leaders of the largest interest groups like to maintain that they are nonpolitical in any partisan sense. At least officially, most of them tend to follow the old rule of Samuel Gompers, who steadfastly refused to have the AFL become a party tool and insisted only on rewarding labor's friends and punishing labor's enemies, regardless of party affiliation. Part of the rationale behind the Gompers viewpoint is that such strategy maximizes a group's bargaining power with both parties. The same interest-group leadership may be consulted by both parties in drafting party-platform statements on a particular subject and may have some members active in the nominations of both parties. In recent years, to be sure, certain interest groups have appeared to align themselves with one or the other of the parties. Yet it is far from clear that either the Republican or the Democratic party has a monopoly of labor, business, agriculture, or any other major interest in American society. One is more apt to find that segments of these interests identify more strongly with one party than another, although these identifications are unstable and will shift from time to time.

The NAACP, one of the most active and controversial of the major interest groups in the present era, has steadfastly refrained from partisan alignment in order to be free to support those candidates most acceptable to their aims in behalf of American Negroes. Their statement in the heat of pre-convention Republican politics in 1964 that their members would not support Senator Barry Goldwater if he were nominated for President was a break with their traditional policy. Nevertheless, it was consistent with the propensity of interest groups in general to maximize their chances of having both parties basically favorable toward their particular aims.[19]

GROUP INTERDICTION OF PARTISAN POLICY-MAKING

Consequently we find political patterns of an enduring sort in which groups and their leaders vie with each other in specific policy areas. To some extent they are constantly competing for a favored position with the party in power, or at least for privileged access to those who head the government. Leaders of the party in power in turn will try to obtain or hold the favorable sentiments of as many of these groups as possible, but as time passes and decisions are made, the party in power must inevitably support some groups more than others. The groups which lose out in this competition will tend to become disaffected and move toward the party out of power. Thus too much affinity for the AFL-CIO may cost a party the support of several segments of independent union members. Similarly, attempts to placate the Farm Bureau may alienate leaders of the Farmers Union as well as of some labor and business organizations.

Since the parties do not have clear control over the Administration and Congress, and since neither of the latter two consistently maintains an internal cohesion, interest group spokesmen frequently find it more profitable and more promptly effective to cultivate those subordinate units of Congress and the Administration dealing directly with a special field of interest. This is done, of course, not just by lobbying in Washington in the conventional sense, but by working at the grassroots among the clientele of the bureau, the constituencies of the legislators, and the mass media which circulate therein. Such action often enables group spokesmen to get results without having to wait for the next election and without expending effort on a broader scale. It also minimizes the group leaders' problems of maintaining control over their own memberships, because they can point to specific, direct attempts at influence without being obliged to carry their memberships into a comprehensive propaganda operation.

In many ways, interest-group leaders are in favorable positions with respect to the party leaders in the American political system. Without relinquishing much autonomy, they can bargain and compete to have one or both of the major parties adopt their special views. If they are unsuccessful with the party in power, they can throw at least some of their support to the opposite party. Even if they do not meet with much success in either party, they still may exploit the subsystems in which they are especially involved. There they can keep a constant and expert vigilance, cultivating bureau and committee leaders, fighting hostile groups, checking positions taken by officials and legislators on issues vital to them, and communicating with the bureau's clientele and the committee members' constituents.

POSSIBILITIES OF PARTY INFLUENCE

How, then, can party leaders—either of the party in power or of the minority party—effectively influence the decisions made in a subsystem? Ideal conditions would exist when the Administration and Congress are dominated by the same majority viewpoint; when they can point to a clear margin of public confidence in the election returns, in editorial comment, and in public opinion polls; and when this sentiment reinforces the control of the Administration over the bureaucracy and the control of the Congress over its committee personnel. Under such conditions, which are rare indeed, there would be in fact party government, and the decisions made in subsystems would be little more than reflections of the general political system. Since situations are usually quite different from this ideal, it is appropriate to attempt to state some of the conditions which are more apt to help maximize party effectiveness in subsystem activity. One such condition exists when there is a close identity of membership between some of the major groups involved in subsystem deliberation and one or

the other of the two major political parties. Thus, one
might expect at least non-Southern Democrats on a
committee to line up more closely with the point of
view expressed by AFL-CIO representatives in a hearing
than would the Republican committee members. The
"party line" emergent in this situation would be partially a product of substantial overlap in organizational
membership between the national Democratic party
and the AFL-CIO.

The same tendency would apply where interest-group
leaders were also party leaders or were closely identified
with leaders of one of the major parties. In such a situation the subsystem battle may likely be enlarged to a
more general partisan struggle, with top leaders in the
Administration and from the Administration's party in
Congress taking up the cudgels, especially if the votes
at stake are many. To illustrate, farm politics took on
unusually strong tinges of party politics during the
Truman Administration's attempt to put across the
Brannan plan, named after the Secretary of Agriculture
at that time. The head of the American Farm Bureau
Federation, Allan B. Kline, led the fight against the
Brannan proposal, which would have altered substantially the existing Hope-Aiken law enacted by a Republican Congress under the joint sponsorship of Representative Clifford R. Hope and Senator George D. Aiken.
Several Democratic congressional spokesmen took to
the hustings to address farm organizations in a counter-
attack against Mr. Kline's views, to pin a Republican
label upon him, and to wean the membership of the
Farm Bureau away from him toward the Democratic
voting column in 1950. Senator Hubert Humphrey told
a Minnesota audience that in the Hope-Aiken plan

there was "little hope and a lot of 'achin'." He urged all farm organizations, including the Farm Bureau, to turn against the Bureau's national leadership as represented by Mr. Kline. The Senator stated that "Allan B. Kline does not represent the wishes of the rank and file of membership of the Farm Bureau," and he added, "Kline just made a bad guess when he thought Dewey would be President."[20]

Reflected in the conditions just cited is another general situation in which the partisan point of view is likely to be imprinted upon the participants in a subsystem. In this situation the issues involved apparently have considerable and increasing relevance for a large segment of the public, so much so as to make them critical factors in the next election. In this kind of situation, a matter which starts out perhaps as a family quarrel among bureaucrats, committee members, and special interests who have long been dealing with such subjects, somehow attracts a larger public and threatens the political equilibrium of the leaders in the parties, the Administration, and the Congress, who then assert their concern. In this way "little policy" can grow into "big policy" and move from subsystem toward system. A word applying to this process has grown out of the slang of the strategists of the Cold War during the 1950's and 1960's—"escalation." When the controversies of a subsystem "escalate," they become matters of major concern for the general political system and for the parties, since they threaten the existing power structure.

Finally, the party point of view can be maintained more effectively if some of the major bureaucratic and legislative participants in a subsystem are in situations in which the party leaders can exercise some sanctions against them or offer them some compensations. In the case of a bureau leader this would be more likely if he were a political appointee of the Administration and if he had hopes of rising in the inner circles of party politics rather than remaining in the bureau. Conversely, a senator or a representative engaged in the activities of a subsystem may show special susceptibility to party influence if he is about to stand for re-election in a two-party state or district where the division is close and where his party offers him the promise of funds, speeches, and publicity.[21]

SUMMARY

The President and the leaders of the Administration, through the more formal factors which make for hierarchical control, may exert influence upon the behavior of bureau leaders and through them affect the pattern of policy-making in the subsystem. Among the major factors of this type are budgetary controls, clearance requirements for proposed legislation, staffing controls, departmental supervision and organization, and restraints on certain types of communications from the bureau to outside groups. All of these factors, however, are limited in their effects; furthermore, though they constitute conditions which in general circumscribe the policy-making autonomy of bureau leaders, they do not necessarily produce strong, authoritative, and detailed policy direction from the top.

An essential ingredient of informal influence of the President and high-echelon leaders in the Administration is their ability to place in the departments and agencies sufficient politically sympathetic people to infuse the intimate environment of bureau leaders with the viewpoints of the Administration. On occasion, these political appointees within the departments are able to offer rewards in the form of favorable decisions, appointments, and the like to bureau leaders in exchange for compliance with the Administration's goals. Conversely, the President and his aides are able to use their power and prestige to threaten bureau leaders who get so far out of line that the Administration's position seems endangered.

The same sort of informal influence sometimes is available to the Administration with regard to congressional committee participants in subsystems, but to much less an extent, since the normative separation of powers tends to minimize the opportunities for the Administration's leaders to develop informal relations with committee leaders. In the case of committee leaders, interpersonal relations appear less crucial than the degree to which the President commands a favorable margin of public sentiment and uses it as a weapon. However, such use of presidential prestige is often limited by the Administration's desire to avoid too-frequent involvement of the symbol of the President. Consequently, it is reserved for major policy battles.

On the whole, the greatest presidential influence over the course of behavior in a subsystem lies via influence over bureau leaders who are strongly oriented toward the Administration personally and whose orientations are reinforced by the hierarchy. Such leaders are apt to assume the role of presidential representatives in the subsystem to a marked degree. Nevertheless, this relationship tends to hold considerable reciprocity, with the Administration depending upon the bureau leaders to exercise initiative and to promote policies which will reflect credit upon the higher echelons.

Centralized influence over the course of behavior in subsystems is exercised even less by congressional leaders than by leaders in the Administration. The autonomy of individual members and of committee leaders in the Senate is especially notable. Although some moves have been made to reduce the number of committees in Congress, to provide more staff with broader capacities, to develop research facilities, to promote joint action between the houses, and to ward off the splintering effects of lobbying, both houses of Congress still maintain diffuse structures for policy-making. They also demonstrate considerable reluctance to force more central discipline. Consequently, leading members of committees and their staffs tend to become the focal points of bureau leaders' attention. They may symbolize Congress for these bureaucrats and command considerable compliance from them, especially when a bureau's leadership is not strongly oriented toward the Administration.

Party leaders can mobilize votes and therefore can exert influence upon the general direction of governmental decisions, but they have to bargain with leaders of groups which specialize in specific types of issues and policies. These groups have the advantages of more cohesive organization and greater ability to concentrate attention on particular issues. Their leaders are able to take advantage of the lesser cohesion of the parties and the relatively weak party control in Congress and the Administration. Group leaders can cultivate bureau and committee leaders dealing directly with their areas of interest, as well as the clientele of the bureau and the constituents of committee members.

Except under conditions in which the Administration and Congress are dominated by the same partisan majority, supported by a sizeable vote of confidence at the polls, the possibilities of party influence on the course of behavior in a subsystem are most likely to depend upon three factors. One factor is the identity of membership between groups interested in the affairs of a particular subsystem and one or the other of the major parties. Another is the degree to which leaders of such groups are also party leaders or are identified closely with leaders of one or the other parties. A third factor is the degree to which a subsystem issue assumes increasing relevance for large segments of the public, making it imperative that party leaders concern themselves with the issue in order to protect themselves at the polls.

CHAPTER FOUR

Relationships
Within the Subsystem:
Part One

We have remarked that a subsystem tends to
have a decisive quality of its own. In other words, within one of these little political worlds the chief participants interact with and react to one another to some
degree independently of the larger political world of
which the subsystem is a part. In so doing, they build
up patterns of influence that are primarily effective in
the limited area of policy-making with which the subsystem is concerned. Yet insofar as the decisions they
reach are not substantially altered by the general political system, the relations among members of a subsystem
are basic determinants of the kind of public policy that
comes into being for that particular substantive area.
Many of the decisions reached in subsystems, though
they be considered minor or detailed or insignificant
when cast individually against a global backdrop, are

collectively the stuff of which a large share of our total public policy is made. Emanating from the interactions of participants frequently characterized by their specialization and sheer staying power, these policies individually may lack the necessary glamor to attract wide interest. Nonetheless, their cumulative importance as well as their specific importance in given areas of American life cannot be disregarded. Hence the processes by which they are determined are crucial.

In depicting relevant aspects of the relations within a subsystem the sections which follow will draw considerably on a study of the subsystem which, to all intents and purposes, shaped United States policy toward American Indians during the period between the pre-New Deal days of 1928 until the late 1940's.[1] By thus projecting from analysis of one subsystem over an extensive time period, it is the author's hope both to lend continuity and cohesiveness to the study and also to produce some propositions which will lead to further exploration and more systematic study of this level of the political process. In this sense the work also may hopefully be regarded as a moderate addition to other studies of policy-making of a kindred type.[2]

The political subsystem of Indian affairs is especially interesting and appropriate to this study for several reasons. One is its comprehensive coverage of the social, political, and economic problems of a small, special subpopulation of the United States. Another is its relative isolation from the mainstream of public knowledge, attention, and sentiment, which lends it an extra degree of autonomy in comparison to some other subsystems. A third reason is that, despite its relative isolation from general public sentiment, this subsystem periodically demonstrates a certain integral quality with regard to the general political setting, and it has long been among the more insistent so-called minor problems on the national scene. The latter characteristic is evidenced in part by the historically interminable nature of the "Indian problem" as it has survived many fundamental national developments and many deliberate devices for eliminating both Indians and special federal Indian programs. Its persistence is also demonstrated by the numerous bills dealing with Indian affairs which are introduced in each Congress. Probably few other so-called little or routine policy areas have been as impregnable to solution or to enforced demise. This political subsystem, which largely decides what the "Great White Father" shall say and do, is a mixture of intensely interacting participants from the Bureau of Indian Affairs, from congressional committees, and from special-interest groups.

Some subsystems are larger than the one chiefly considered here; others are smaller. Some cover much narrower considerations of policy; others cover much broader and more comprehensive ones. In his recent consideration of two types of "sub-governments" as examples of the large and the small, Cater chose the defense policy-making system as the large extreme and the "two-man" system for setting sugar import quotas as the small one.[3] Obviously, there is much yet to be learned from the study of such different types of subsystems. Size and complexity of variables call for comparative research. If this short study leads to further work on these lines, so much the better.

STRATEGIES AND INFLUENCE OF
BUREAU PERSONNEL IN THE SUBSYSTEM

In the web of relationships of the subsystem, bureau leaders occupy strategic positions and usually play roles as leaders in the policy-making process by a variety of means of influence. Central to their functioning as makers of policy is their ability ultimately to affect the committee members, who in turn will presumably get their respective legislative bodies to act more or less in accordance with their recommendations. Yet as the following discussion will bear out, although the most important ultimate focal points of bureau leaders' efforts in policy-making are the committee leaders and members, the means of reaching these points are diverse and often indirect. Furthermore, although the committee members have much official power in policy matters, their political wills are particularly sensitive to the opinions of other key participants in the subsystem, a fact which bureau leaders often can exploit, yet which sometimes works against them.

In utilizing the various modes of influence, the bureau leader's degree of strategic sensitivity is significant in his capacity to evoke favorable responses from legislative committees as well as from public groups. By "strategic sensitivity" is meant the bureau leader's ability to anticipate or to recognize the expectations of committee members, to gauge the timeliness of a request, and to be cognizant of the claims, demands, and expectations which others direct at committee members immediately, but which are ultimately directed at the bureau itself. Psychologists might call this the "ability to take the role of the other." Specialists in communications analysis might term this some form of feedback. Essentially, it involves the ability of the bureau spokesman to understand the pertinent conditions under which the legislator is going to receive and react to suggestions from a bureaucrat. The bureaucrat needs to understand the degree to which a legislator desires to protect his representative role and also to protect his own prestige as well as that of his legislative colleagues. A bureau leader needs to be able to assess danger signals flashed by committee members when they feel that their relations with their constituents are being threatened. Moreover, he must understand the sets of interests and opinions that committee members are most likely to be receptive to in different situations. Without some of this kind of talent, a bureau leader is likely to be ineffective in policy leadership.

USING TOP-LEVEL SUPPORT

The proposals of bureau leaders in a subsystem can be either endorsed or mediated by the higher echelons of the Administration of which the bureau is a part, especially in major issues of policy where the points under consideration are crucial to the Administration. In such an instance, the head of the department and other top leaders are likely to become involved in a fashion analogous to the previously described intervention of the President. Of course, the rule of limited intervention in lower echelon affairs usually applies to the Secretary and other top leaders of a department, as well as to the President, although in lesser degree. The Secretary does not intervene in every skirmish between one of his bureaus and a congressional committee any more than the President intervenes in every battle between a department and congressional leaders. Leaders of the Administration can be "supporting artillery" for a bureau chief, and the more crucial the target, the larger the "gun" that is brought to bear upon it.

The effect of the use of this strategy by a bureau leader was generally illustrated in the legislative relations of the Bureau of Indian Affairs during the New Deal, when high-level support from the Administration seemed to enhance the ability of the Bureau's leaders to gain acceptance of their recommendations and to defend themselves against attacks from committees and interest groups. During the earlier years of the New Deal, Commissioner Collier of the Bureau was successful on numerous occasions in getting Secretary of the Interior Ickes to communicate with or to testify before committees of Congress in support of the Bureau's viewpoint. In these instances the Secretary made the Commissioner's battles his own, with the characteristic Ickes vigor, and he usually helped to subdue critical committee members.

As has already been indicated, this state of mutual reinforcement does not appear uniformly in the relations of bureaus with the Administration. Yet every bureau chief to some degree has a choice as to the extent to which his efforts will be identified with the goals of the Administration and a choice as to how much he will exploit the power symbolized by the Secretary of his department or by the President. The case of Collier, Ickes, and Roosevelt was extreme, perhaps, in two ways: first, in the long span of their simultaneous incumbencies in office and second, in the degree of their interest and ideological proximity. All three men saw the New Deal through from its inception. All three were committed to the "progressive" point of view, sometimes looking with disdain upon the conventional political parties, but always strong for the "New Deal party."[4] Ickes was put forward at first for the office of Commissioner of Indian Affairs under the New Deal, at which time he was supported by Collier and others. Roosevelt instead selected Ickes—almost sight unseen—to be Secretary of the Interior. Forthwith, Ickes, the party maverick in the Cabinet, gained the President's support and confidence, something he succeeded generally in holding for the next twelve years. The Secretary in turn got Roosevelt to appoint Collier as Commissioner, beginning a similar pattern of relations between the Bureau chief and the Department head. This was reinforced by the interest in Indians held by Anna Willmarth Ickes, the Secretary's first wife, and by her assistance to Collier.

The Commissioner followed the strategy of using the backing of these leaders of the Administration to a maximum degree, and in turn utilized his own talents for promoting the New Deal in areas not particularly germane to his own Bureau. In securing the passage of the comprehensive Indian Reorganization Act of 1934, the Commissioner obtained the close support of the Secretary plus two endorsements from the President. He also used the prestige of the President in explaining the purposes of the bill to Indians in Oklahoma, telling them:

> You know that at the present time President Roosevelt controls both Houses of Congress. When the President wants a piece of legislation, he gets it from Congress. The bill we are going to discuss today is an Administration measure. It is a President Roosevelt

measure. The majority of the members of Congress do not pretend to understand the Indian question in detail at all. The majority of the members of Congress have nothing to gain or lose by any Indian legislation. In other words, if the Administration had wanted to put this bill through quietly and quickly, understand they had the power, and they have the power to do it. The Administration, as I stated before, has adopted a new policy, which is the policy of bringing all the Indians into consultation on the bill, even though it entails, or may entail delay.[5]

Needless to say, many committee members do not appreciate bureaucratic attempts to exploit the halo which sometimes attends presidential leadership, especially when the bureau spokesman infers that Congress can be pushed around by a strong President. Senator Elmer Thomas berated Collier for making the above statement. He said:

> You told *my* Indians down at *my* home that it made no difference what Congress thought about it, that you would pass the bill if you wanted to, and would do it quickly.[6]

Also at issue here was another legislative norm: the sanctity of the local state or district against "outside" interference, especially "meddling" by the executive branch without consulting the lawmaker from that constituency. In using presidential support in this way the Commissioner evidently chose to bet that, given the popularity of the President, the exploitation of his support would in the long run more than offset the hostility aroused in the Senate Committee by violating some of the norms of its members. In this case the bill was passed, although Senator Thomas succeeded in delaying its application to his Indians in Oklahoma until he personally could investigate the need for it.

In the years between the advent of the New Deal and the advent of World War II the Commissioner secured the support of the Secretary in many other situations despite Ickes's preoccupation with Public Works and with the rarefied intrigues around the President. For example, Collier got the Secretary to issue a memorandum to Bureau employees telling them, in effect, either to quit criticizing the new policies in Indian affairs or to resign, and that if they persisted in their criticism without resigning, they would be dismissed.[7] The Commissioner also cited the Secretary in standing up against congressional criticism of Indian Bureau publicity tactics and of the use of an official Indian Service periodical to organize support for the new policies. Collier told members of the House Committee on Indian Affairs:

> . . . We are promoting many things which, for their success depend upon a friendly and informed opinion. We should properly cultivate public opinion, and we will continue to do that.
>
> I need only to add that I think this committee ought to know by this time that neither Secretary Ickes nor I hesitate to speak. We can always put out a release and we do so.[8]

The two officials also joined in fighting certain groups which brought charges against them before the Dies Committee on Un-American Activities and before the Senate Committee on Indian Affairs. They also joined in warding off constant attempts to repeal the Indian Reorganization Act or to undermine it by cutting its appropriations. The Commissioner in turn extended his activities to take part not only in the propaganda battle in behalf of the President's Supreme Court plan, but also in the early attempts to counter the growth of the America First movement, two courses of action which reinforced strong interests of the Secretary's as well as of the President's.[9]

In thus identifying with and using the endorsements of the Administration "above and beyond the call of duty," the Commissioner was often able to maximize his influence in the subsystem of Indian affairs by associating his recommendations with the prestige of higher officials. At the same time, however, he enlarged the range of controversy in the subsystem, and both he and his Bureau were recipients of retaliations that otherwise might not have come their way.

The other side of the coin of a bureau leader's attachment to higher symbols in the Administration and his exploitation of their prestige was demonstrated later when the support of Roosevelt and Ickes for Collier's Bureau was not so easily obtained and when it was not so effective, even though obtained. The Bureau headquarters were moved to Chicago during World War II to make room in Washington for wartime activities. Close communications with the Department of Interior and the White House were severely curtailed. The attention of the Administration was turned almost entirely from domestic policy to the war. In fact, it was doubtful if the New Deal was at that time the basis of the Administration's support so much as was the unifying objective of defense and victory.

During this period the Bureau chief became increasingly unable to stave off attacks from congressional committees. He was able to help the Bureau survive, but little else. Part of his difficulty in keeping committee members interested in Indian welfare and rehabilitation arose from the temporary mitigation of his Bureau's problems by the increase in Indian income due to wartime employment and by the relief furnished by the money sent home by many Indian servicemen. Part of the Commissioner's difficulty with some committees came from long-standing personal differences. Yet a crucial factor was his record of consistent fighting for the views of the New Deal and the use of the Administration's power to protect the policies installed in Indian affairs early in the New Deal. Lacking the continued strong reciprocal support of the Administration during the war period, the Commissioner was no longer able to maintain a favorable equilibrium.[10]

LEGISLATIVE LIAISON

In any case, bureau leaders do not depend exclusively upon mediation of their influence through the topmost levels of the Administration, or upon calling down specific presidential or departmental blessings upon their efforts. The dynamic relations of the subsystem are much more diverse and frequently more routine. For example, many matters are handled through "organizational" channels of legislative liaison, primarily involving some members of the legal and liaison staffs of both department and bureau, plus the staffs of committees in Congress. This staff routinization of bureau-committee relations has increased over the years as a corollary of the general increase in organizational provisions for executive–legislative relations, since administrators have realized anew the importance of the political context in which they work. Departments now maintain legislative liaison divisions headed by top-level officials, staffed with extensive legal and political talent, and sometimes even maintaining offices on the Hill. Usually, certain specialists within a department from this section or from a Chief Counsel's or Solicitor's office work closely with bureau and committee leaders in drafting proposed legislation, in arranging testimony for investigations, and in communicating to the committees the day-to-day views of the bureau, and vice versa. This part of the process is most effective, on the whole, for dealing with the extensive number of routine requests which come to legislators and which they pass on to executive units for expediting or for explanation.[11]

However, it is also the case that embedded in the formal legislative liaison structure will very likely be some individuals who are unusually important adjuncts to the efforts of bureau leaders to influence policy. A person of this sort often combines legal talent, political sagacity, and knowledge of the substance of the policy. Such a person may be a top legal aide of a bureau or he may be attached to a department's staff and assigned to work on a bureau's problems. Usually his formal status is less significant than his informal function. A prototype of this was the late Felix Cohen, who served the Interior Department and the Bureau of Indian Affairs during the New Deal and later. He was not only the outstanding researcher on the law of Indian affairs, but an active participant in the decisions of the Bureau, both on policy proposals and on policy interpretations, as well as a man possessed of considerable acquaintance with the group politics of Indian affairs.

A different variety of the so-called Washington lawyer involved in legislative liaison was dramatically portrayed in the Army-McCarthy hearings in 1954 in which the role of the Army Counsel was explored. Such a staff member serves essentially as a link between committee leaders and departmental and bureau leaders. He inevitably is called upon to live in two camps since he spends a large portion of his time actually with committee members and staff; yet his reference points are supposed to be the administrative agency and its bureaus. The role of such a person is to interpret the views of the committee leaders to bureau and department officials to prevent the administrative units from incurring congressional animosity, and at the same time to cultivate receptivity in the committees for the viewpoints of the administrative units, as well as to serve department and bureau heads as a strategic counsellor in dealing with legislative groups.

INTERPERSONAL INFLUENCE

Perhaps the most difficult pattern of bureaucratic influence in the subsystem to assess is that mediated by the informal, interpersonal relations of bureau leaders with committee leaders and interest-group leaders. Aspects of these relations can be gleaned from diaries, case studies, and memoirs. Occasionally, the relationship is apparent in the friendly or hostile sentiments which accompany the record-conscious testimony at hearings. Much of it lies off the record, but perhaps may be clarified in due time as research in this area is developed.

There are some indications that bureau leaders and influential committee members are sometimes considerably encouraged either in espousing proposals or in blocking them on the basis of these personal relationships. Certainly there is a tendency to blame discord on "differences in personality" or to credit success to "personal friendship." For example, John Collier spent several years as a spokesman for the American Indian Defense Association prior to his own appointment as Commissioner, working intimately with members and staff of the House and Senate Committees on Indian Affairs. Collier's personal influence was accredited by Commissioner Charles H. Burke, head of the Bureau under the Coolidge Administration, with being a key factor in starting a Senate investigation of the Bureau and of Burke's administration in 1928. In the period from 1928 to 1932 Collier established close relations with the counsel of the Senate Committee and with Congressman Edgar Howard, chairman of the House Committee, which subsequently appeared to help Collier in the early stages of his own tenure as Commissioner after 1933.

On the other hand, as time went by there were some indications that interpersonal relations were minimized as factors determining the ability of the Commissioner to influence committee leaders in subsystem policymaking. Several of the old Senate Committee "friends," who were somewhat favorably disposed toward Collier before his appointment in 1933, subsequently regarded him as "no longer having the same point of view" and as "having become like the rest of the bureaucrats." In other words, as time passed the different orientations and role requirements of committee members and of bureau leaders seemed to exert a progressively negative effect upon the personal relationships between the Commissioner and his committee friends. Whether this would have been the case had the Commissioner been less inclined to be oriented generally toward the Ad-

ministration is another matter. It is possible that a bureau chief who did not identify so strongly with the
Administration and did not see his job particularly as
involving enterprise for the executive branch, not only
might have maintained but also might have enhanced
his personal channels of influence with legislators in the
subsystem.

In another phase of the subsystem the Commissioner
succeeded in maintaining his friendly interpersonal relations with the leaders of a major interest group with
whom he had associated prior to taking office. Some of
this was accomplished by "institutionalizing" the interpersonal relationships, that is, by bringing associates
from this group into posts in the Bureau or by establishing semiformal advisory relationships with them. On
the other hand, some erstwhile friends from other
groups turned against the Commissioner when they did
not receive a similar reception from the Bureau after
Collier took office, and almost uniformly they tried to
defeat Collier's policies. Throughout Collier's tenure
some of the strongest support from interest groups for
his views vis-à-vis the Committees came from that group
in which interpersonal relationships had been most
strongly reinforced by institutionalization.[12]

CHOOSING ALTERNATIVE COMMITTEES

Among the strategies of influence which a bureau
leader can use is that of playing one committee against
another. Every bureau deals with at least four committees of Congress, and frequently with more than four,
giving the bureau leader a range of alternatives along
this line. We have already observed the tendencies of
the Senate Appropriations Committee to counterbal-

ance the House Appropriations Committee. In addition, appropriations committees can and do alter policies enacted by substantive committees, both in setting the amount of money available for authorized programs and in altering the conditions under which money can be spent by the administrative unit. It is also possible that one investigating committee may counteract another in inquiries covering much of the same ground. All of these situations furnish possibilities in strategy for bureau leaders.

The last of these possibilities was used with some success by Commissioner Collier in the early 1940's. At that time the Investigating Subcommittee of the Senate Committee on Indian Affairs, which had been operating since 1928, brought out one of its most damaging indictments of the Bureau's policies and personnel. Shortly thereafter the Commissioner arranged with the leaders of the House Committee on Indian Affairs for a subcommittee of that unit also to investigate the Bureau, limiting its probe to specific, mutually acceptable points of inquiry to be covered in a stated length of time. Largely under the direction of Congressman Karl Mundt this was done, and a report was published which was considerably at variance with the Senate Subcommittee's report. Temporarily, the Bureau received some respite from the hostility emanating from the Senate Committee on Indian Affairs.[13]

EXPLOITING COMMITTEE HEARINGS

Despite recognizable limitations, committee hearings furnish important channels of influence for participants in a subsystem, especially for bureau leaders. It is true that publicity, which recently has increasingly been

turned upon hearings and which may become fiercer as
new mass-communications techniques are exploited,
often makes the participants more like actors on a stage
than discussants in a conference. Long before television,
in fact, committee members, administrative officials,
and group representatives tended to speak for the record
and for the press. Yet hearings are likely to be less
formal, despite some of the conditions under which
they are held, than congressional debates, public addresses, or long-range battles via press releases. Most
hearings, especially those which are not televised and
which are not given extensive press coverage, provide opportunities for some relatively unguarded communication among the policy-makers of the subsystem, as well
as the opportunity to extend and exploit the proceed-
ings for propaganda purposes.

Bureau leaders can frequently build up an impressive
case for their side in the record. This furnishes docu-
mentation for those committee members who would be
inclined to argue for the bureau's viewpoint, either in
executive session where committee votes are taken, before the whole legislative body, or in public speeches.
On occasion, a strong presentation in a hearing by bureau leaders may influence neutral or less-involved committee members. Yet often the most vital factors in
communications in committee hearings, as in other
small-group assemblages, are the methods and the disposition of the communicator plus his listeners' atti-
tudes toward him and what he symbolizes, rather than
the alleged facts presented and the logic used. Thus,
among busy committee members who do not like to
be snowed under by official or technical talk, bureau
spokesmen can, by the strategies they employ, create

or reinforce in the hearings sentiments about themselves and their organizations which have a lasting and controlling effect on the decisions of committees. It may be most important to the legislator whether he feels that the bureaucrat: (1) "knows what he's talking about" (e.g., speaks with confidence, answers questions simply and often categorically); (2) "plays it straight" (e.g., does not appear to evade, admits to imperfection, keeps the committee informed); and (3) "cooperates" (e.g., seems amenable to suggestions from committee members, shows them proper deference, does not try to put them on the spot with the press or with their constituents, and does not play his initiative too heavy-handedly).

To make a maximum effect upon committee members in hearings, bureau leaders must be capable of exploiting their public impact in order partly to overcome the innate advantage held by committee leaders and staff members, who define the boundaries and the ground rules. The scheduling of witnesses, the pre-structuring of questions to be asked, and the timing and control of publicity are crucial to the pace, content, and general impression which the hearing leaves, both upon the public and upon the participants. In all these, committee leaders and staff members tend to have the upper hand, and they try to maintain this control because they are quite sensitive to the opinion of certain audiences. They want hearings controlled so that they will be aware of who constitutes their audience and what their audience will hear.

Yet complete control is impossible, and the committee members' means of assessing the actual nature and extent of public impact are naturally limited. For example, even though they do not know to what extent the rank and file members of certain groups in their constituencies will be influenced by a bureau chief's testimony in a hearing, his potential ability to influence some constituents can have its effect on committee members. Committee members may have similar reactions to publicity given a bureaucrat's testimony in the press and other mass media, even if it appears only in certain Washington and New York newspapers which may be inconsequential in the legislator's home state. This gives rise to the interesting possibility that congressmen, insofar as they are uncertain about mass opinion back home, frequently are most immediately affected by the opinions of their peers and of prestigeful newspapers. It may also be that people who deal in public relations and live by public opinion are overly inclined to think that all people are as much involved in the game as are the most sensitive few. Mass-opinion studies would indicate that most people are not so intimately affected by the subtleties of mass communications; nevertheless this does not necessarily change political leaders' conceptions of how publicity has its effect.

THE USE OF PUBLICITY

In addition to the opportunities for making news in committee hearings, there are other important facets of publicity (or propaganda) activities of bureau leaders which are critical. In general, these practices are natural outgrowths of needs for certain types of communications in our political system and overall legal attempts to limit them have been impracticable. Consequently there are usually abundant opportunities for bureau leaders to exploit the media of mass communication. A bureau's information office regularly gives out press releases (usually under departmental auspices) which, while dealing mainly with the facts of the bureau's business, nevertheless furnish a means of keeping the organization and its officials constantly on the news wires. If the bureau chief has an exceptional item to give out, he can usually get a reporter's ear without difficulty. From time to time radio and television opportunities come his way, as well as requests to write articles. Also, there is usually a network of friendly media only too willing to help carry the propaganda battle for the bureau leaders, to serve as vehicles of semiofficial tests of public sentiment, and to be favored in turn with inside stories. Finally, there is the array of official publications and reports, many of which can serve not only as information devices but as media supporting the bureau's policies and goals.[14]

This propaganda battle has an effect on the decisions of the participants in the subsystem, even though it is recognized as an exchange of public-relations missiles. Just as in the case of committee hearings, in the constant public-relations battles of a subsystem the highly active participants are sensitive to the images which they believe others will hold of them as a result of mass communications. In a sense, people in public affairs become (or perhaps always have been) acutely sensitive to their press clippings. Being concerned with maintaining a certain public image, they often act in accordance with or react to the image they perceive to be projected of themselves in publicity and propaganda.

The bureau leader may not have to propagandize a tremendous number of people in order to have an effect. First, the general public is not usually consistently in-

terested in a subsystem. Second, the leading participants
—committee members, clientele leaders, group leaders,
and bureau employees—are the ones who are most sen-
sitized to the propaganda of the subsystem. This means
first that general-circulation media can usually be effectively used only to condition in a general, nontechnical
way the sentiments of the public at large and their
leaders toward the affairs of the subsystem, and second
that "trade" or special-audience media will usually be
more effective in mobilizing and sustaining the sentiments of the "insiders" or the informed and interested
publics of the subsystem and their leaders.

In the publicity battle of Indian affairs, Commissioner Collier had either access to or considerable support from the following: *Indians at Work*, an official
periodical of the Bureau in which he frequently edi-
torialized about current issues of policy; the publications
of the American Indian Defense Association, of which
Collier had formerly been executive director, and the
publications of its successor, the Association on American Indian Affairs; and *The Nation* and *New Republic*,
two liberal periodicals which frequently devoted space
to articles by friends of the New Deal Indian program.
Also, *Collier's* magazine occasionally presented articles
by feature writers who tended to convey the Bureau's
viewpoint in popularized form, and *The New York
Times* and *The Washington Post*, in giving comprehensive coverage to national events, would devote space
occasionally to Commissioner Collier's program. Moreover, releases from the Commissioner's office were sometimes printed in those local Western newspapers whose
readers were likely to be involved. The above types of
publicity were supplemented from time to time with

various articles and addresses by the Commissioner. The Bureau and its chief were unusually well-fortified for the propaganda battle both among the general public and within the limited public of the subsystem.

There were counterparts of the Bureau's channels of publicity and propaganda in which the opposition could have its say—with the notable exception of official Bureau publications. Naturally enough, it was over the use of official publications that Collier had some of his greatest difficulty with committee members and with hostile group leaders. Frequently, they took statements from the Bureau's periodicals and introduced them as examples of unfair or unwarranted use of public facilities and of official status. Committee members warned Collier against such tactics, and subsequently on several occasions members took the matter of the Commissioner's publicity activities to the floor of the House or the Senate. Collier declined to alter his publicity activities, stating that he would never "hesitate to speak out." As a result, his capacity for exploiting the means of publicity seemed to reinforce his immediate influence in the subsystem; however, it also fed a smouldering resentment among those committee members who perceived him as "a good propagandist but a poor Commissioner," and it probably contributed to their increased opposition to Collier in the long run.[15]

CHAPTER FIVE

Relationships
Within the Subsystem:
Part Two

INTERACTIONS BETWEEN BUREAU LEADERS AND GROUPS

Bureau leaders so often take the initiative in drafting and proposing policy changes that they must come to the committees of Congress buttressed by the favorable sentiments of significant groups represented in the subsystem, or at least of the spokesmen for these groups. The groups usually most intimately concerned with the affairs of a subsystem by virtue of their internal relationship with the bureau are its employees and its so-called clientele. Though the two are distinguishable, they often have much in common. In the first place, both depend upon the bureau: the employee for his livelihood and for other job-related satisfactions and the client for services, goods, or direction. Both in some measure are concerned about the organization's rules, goals, and resources. They are further likely to share certain loyalties, to have established certain particular mutual friendships, and perhaps to have identified with common symbols peculiar to that area of policy. Both groups will "know the lingo" of the organization, just as veterans come to know about the certificates of eligibility handled by Veterans Administration employees, or as both farm leaders and Agriculture Department personnel are conversant about parity and price supports. Finally, it is often the case that many employees of a bureau were, or are, clients as well.

Of course, neither the interests of clientele nor those of employees are uniform, and most bureau leaders are content to get major segments of each group, or perhaps only the most vocal ones to concur. This amount of employee and clientele support is well-nigh the crucial minimum for a bureau chief's success in dealing with committees. If he seems to lead and to represent these two groups, his case is likely to carry considerable weight with committee members, other things being equal, because the legislators often view the employees and the clients as considerable molders of what may be called the grass-roots sentiment in their constituencies as well as people who "know what it's all about." The employees are regarded as molders of sentiment partially because they represent the official side of the subsystem in the field. Often they can deliberately help (or fail to help) friends of committee members in the course of the performance of their duties for the bureau. Similarly, clientele leaders will be regarded as opinion molders insofar as they can voice satisfaction or dissatisfaction for the "folks back home" to hear.

Bureau attempts to mobilize employee support do not

meet with uniform success, however. Committee members are likely to be highly suspicious of testimony or opinions conveyed to them under what appears to be some organized campaign from bureau headquarters. Furthermore, groups of employees themselves are likely to resist official attempts to coerce them. The case of the previously mentioned order handed down by Secretary Ickes at Commissioner Collier's request, directing employees of the Indian Bureau to refrain from criticizing new policies, was subsequently aired before a committee by certain unhappy employees, and it was used to cast the shadow of bureaucratic coercion over expressions of opinion by Bureau personnel. The cry of "gag rule" leveled at leaders of the bureaucracy has seldom helped their standing with legislators, and in this instance Ickes and Collier appeared to lose status.

Similarly, bureau leaders usually have to be circumspect about organizing the clientele. Congressmen resent this kind of "public relations," especially in their own territories, and more especially if they are not parties to it. Usually the clientele groups are sufficiently diverse so that some of the clientele who are opposed to the bureau will see to it that committee members are kept well-informed of their views as well as of the opinion-forming operations of the bureaucrats.

The whole problem of the extent of administrative funneling of opinion is highlighted—especially in bureaus which have extensive field organizations—where the promotion of acceptance of policies already approved by Congress gets intermixed with other less-settled goals. Interpretations of rules can themselves be bureaucratic rewards or penalties. Furthermore, it is difficult for the bureaucrat to say where "implementation" stops and "policy proposal" starts. The so-called political aspects of a speech to a clientele or employee group may be toned down, but the opportunity remains to sow the seeds of future support for a hoped-for change in policy. If a bureau leader succeeds in shaping considerable clientele support in the home districts of committee members, he is likely to have some success in getting a favorable vote in the committee, but he is also likely to incur considerable animosity. He may evoke enough immediate sentiment in his behalf to make the legislators feel constrained to pass his proposal. Yet he may create a gnawing resentment which subsequently may be exhibited in retaliatory acts by committee leaders and by clientele and field employees alike.

RELATIONS BETWEEN BUREAU LEADERS AND NON-INTERNAL GROUPS

All groups participating in a subsystem are not necessarily so "internal" to the bureau as are the employees and the clientele. There are likely to be those who are simply in sympathy with the interests of the clientele and the services performed by the bureau. Others are likely to be in competition with or hostile to the clientele. In Indian affairs, a variety of non-Indian groups took interest in the policies of the Bureau apparently because they were primarily concerned about the welfare and the future of Indians as underprivileged people. Of course, other motives may have stirred their members, such as a desire to be socially active, to do good, to be identified with charitable enterprise, and so forth. Nevertheless, these groups were noted for their concern with the problem generally stated as "Indian welfare" or "Indian rights" or "Indian rehabilitation." Yet, despite this general bond of interest these groups often disagreed. For example, church and missionary groups felt that some Indian welfare organizations took too secular an attitude toward the definition of Indian advancement. However, all groups of the welfare type tended to oppose those groups which competed with Indian economic interests or which were actively engaged in trying to pry Indians loose from some of their property or privileges.

To a considerable extent, those non-clientele groups which were sympathetic toward the Bureau's clientele as a class were possessed of what may be called a cosmopolitan outlook. They drew their values from rather universal systems of ethics which were not generated primarily by particular relationships within the subsystem. They had memberships composed of people from diverse geographic and occupational categories. Some of their strongest bonds seemed to be ideological. On the other hand, the groups competing with the Indians or hostile toward the Bureau's protection of its clientele frequently seemed to be what may be characterized as more local or grass-roots in nature. Their systems of values arose from particular situations in "Indian Country." Their objectives were largely economic advantage for themselves and their kind, and their bonds were often geographic or occupational.

In gaining support for his policy views—especially to get backing before the congressional committees—the Commissioner of Indian Affairs found the cosmopolitan groups more amenable to his ideological approach. Insofar as his philosophy appealed to them, these groups were likely to support his concrete plans. The catch was, of course, that cosmopolitan groups lacked to some extent the ingredients for affecting non-Indian sentiment at the grass-roots where committee members might most likely be touched via the ballot box. Of course, cosmopolitan groups did have considerable field contact with Indians, with whom they could often make their views felt, but Indian opinion was often not the controlling one in a Western constituency, and most Committee of Indian Affairs members were from the West. Cosmopolitan groups were usually more skilled and effective in the battle of the mass media, the hearing room, and the colloquium than in the battle for local votes.

On the other hand, the local, anti-protection groups were usually less amenable to the Commissioner's views and were more likely to oppose him before the legislative committees as long as his major efforts were to guard energetically the economic interests of his clientele and to promote extensively their security through government aid. Frequently it was possible for leaders of these groups to convince committee members that they carried great weight in Western constituencies, since their memberships included more non-Indians of the West. Moreover, it was often characteristic of some grass-roots organizations that they would adopt ideological positions which would question basically the integrity of Bureau leaders and the philosophy behind their programs. Characteristic of the ideological warfare waged by these more extreme local interests was a weaving of examples of the Bureau's red tape and statements and actions of officials taken largely out of context into a pattern of interpretive innuendo. The result of this attack against the Bureau, somewhat irrespective of its intent or content, was basically to reduce congressional and public confidence in the Bureau's policies and personnel. To some extent this made it easier to assert local non-Indian interests over against those of Indians as seen by the Bureau, as well as to add strength to the anti-Administration forces in general. In fact, the more extreme members of certain of these local groups built up a considerable record of association with the more rabid, "super-patriotic," isolationist groups which fought the emerging internationalism of the New Deal from 1937 to 1941. Their compatibility reached a zenith, perhaps, when Hitler's government proclaimed that American Indians were Aryans. However, this particular collection of extremists in Indian affairs subsided somewhat after their money-raising operations among Indians were criticized, and after the isolationist movement subsided during World War II.[1]

INVOLVEMENT OF GROUPS IN POLICY DETERMINATION BY BUREAU LEADERS

In dealing with groups, both clientele and non-clientele, bureau leaders may exercise a practice that is common to many forms of so-called administrative public relations today. Selznick in his study of the TVA deals extensively with one form of this technique under the nomenclature of cooptation.[2] In other forms it is called *consultation* or the *advisory process*. Administrators in the field of public education frequently speak of *lay-participation* or the *participatory process*. Essentially, the procedure is one of calling upon members of groups outside the organization to share in the study, planning, discussion, promotion, or application of its policies. The general idea is frequently justified by administrators on the ground that the people concerned about an organization's activities should share in its policy-making.

They also believe, but are perhaps somewhat reluctant to affirm outside the walls of their profession, that this is an excellent device for building political support for the organization and for those parts of its program which are deemed most important by its leaders.

In the Bureau of Indian Affairs cooptation and lay-participation were well-exemplified in the Commissioner's conferences with Indian groups. Also in the preparation of the Indian Reorganization Act, he and his associates held a large-scale conference in Washington attended by a variety of specialists, particularly anthropologists and interest-group spokesmen, who later supported the new program enthusiastically. The *institutionalization* of personal relationships previously referred to in Chapter Four was still another variety of cooptation. In promoting the Bureau's policies before congressional committees, a good share of the favorable testimony came from spokesmen thus drawn into the Bureau's orbit. Conversely, leaders of groups left outside the orbit tended to be the most persistent and vocal critics of the Bureau's point of view. Frequently they secured the favor of many committee members who viewed the cooptative activity of the Commissioner as improper and who felt it constituted a threat to the legislator's prerogatives. Yet a committee member occasionally responded favorably to an opportunity to be a joint partner with the Commissioner and other Bureau leaders in a swing through the legislator's home state to confer with clientele and group leaders. Thus the legislator could protect his status, or perhaps even increase it, as the man the home folks could count on to get the Bureau to do what they desired. Of course, in the process of such a tour the Bureau leaders often found an opportunity to do "missionary work" of their own, both with the committee members and with his constituents.

STRATEGIES AND INFLUENCE OF COMMITTEE PERSONNEL IN THE SUBSYSTEM

Before inquiring into the ways in which committees and their leaders and staff can influence the course of decisions in a subsystem it is appropriate first to direct attention again briefly to the broad sanctions which committees can effectively wield against bureaus. These grow out of the legislative branch's ability to withhold or provide the resources and the authority essential both to the bureau's operations and to those of the Administration of which the bureau is a part. Because of the decentralized character of Congress, it is the committees' responsibility to make the basic recommendations concerning resources and authority to be allocated to the various bureaus, and these recommendations more often than not are chief determinants of the final congressional acts. This important function of committees and their leaders is the basic ingredient of their influence in the subsystem.

SHAPING BUREAUCRATIC APPLICATION OF LAWS

This influence extends of course beyond the legislative enactment of policies into the administrative interpretation, refinement, and application of laws. Since bureau leaders know that they will have to return repeatedly to the committees for renewals of their resources and for modifications of their authority, they usually try to follow, within reason, the intent of committee members who shaped a given law. This responsiveness of bureau leaders to the wishes and thoughts of committee members extends even to bureau field organization. For example, the leaders of the Bureau of Indian Affairs periodically have changed their plans to abolish or to transfer some field offices because of protests registered by senior committee members who felt unhappy over the prospect of having federal installations removed from their home states or districts.

Much of the intervention of committee members in administrative matters is of one piece with the day-to-day legislative liaison of a bureau. Requests which come to a legislator's office may be referred through his staff to the staff of the bureau. Many of these are routine and are disposed of through settled procedures. Exceptional requests may give rise to discussion among staff members from the bureau, from a committee, and from individual legislators' offices. The ranking committee staff member, acting more or less in behalf of the chairman and other senior committee members (whom he may or may not have consulted), may play an influential role in the determination of the bureau's course of action.

For coverage of this topic in greater detail and with many more examples, Joseph P. Harris's book, previously cited, is especially appropriate.[3] Also, the recent comprehensive study of the legislative process by William J. Keefe and Morris S. Ogul has a most useful chapter thoroughly probing the literature on this subject.[4] And the work of Peter Woll, following somewhat in the footsteps of Charles Hyneman, is also most helpful, especially from the point of view of our constitutional institutions.[5]

BEHAVIOR AND INFLUENCE OF SUBSTANTIVE
COMMITTEE PARTICIPANTS

Senior substantive committee members on a day-to-day, year-in-year-out basis constitute about the most persistent congressional elite engaged in shaping the policies of a bureau. Along with the committee staff, whom the senior members and especially the committee chairman select and work with, they can write substantial amounts of the final versions of policies for a bureau to administer. They do not, in current practice, initiate nearly as many major policy proposals as do the leaders of the bureau, but they largely determine the disposition of the bureau's propositions. In determining the general subject, the duration, and the admission of evidence into hearings, they frequently demonstrate tendencies to give attention and support to those points of view and those groups which reinforce their own positions.

For example, in the passage of the Indian Reorganization Act during the New Deal, the nature of the power of senior committee members was clarified. Although leaders from the Bureau of Indian Affairs presented the Senate Committee with a fifty-two-page bill drafted chiefly by Bureau leaders, and although many principles of that original proposition were finally adopted, the Chairman of the Senate Committee and other senior members exercised considerable censorship over the final product. For instance, Senators Elmer Thomas and Henry F. Ashurst both asked and received major exemptions for their respective states. Furthermore, the final Committee version was substantially determined by Chairman Burton K. Wheeler, who deleted many parts, condensed others, and reportedly told Bureau leaders what would or would not be allowed.[6]

Beyond the individual committee personalities, the major enduring social characteristics of the membership of substantive committees dealing with a particular area of policy are helpful to an understanding of the members' behavior in policy-making. Many standing legislative committees tend, in varying degrees, to attract over the years a predominance of legislators with certain common backgrounds and with certain common values. This happens sometimes, no doubt, because these legislators are anxious to serve on committees dealing with interests of their constituents. It may also occur partly because the legislators themselves are largely products of the subcultures in which they have achieved political success, and their personal preferences and attraction to problems may reflect this environmental conditioning. For whatever the reason, the factors are important ones for which to look in an attempt to understand long-term trends in the patterns of a subsystem. The predominant social conditioning of substantive committee members may help explain the propensity of legislative committees for favoring a particular ideology, a particular region, or a particular segment of the population.

Even looking only at the nature of constituency as indicated by certain general features of the state from which committee members hail and at the length of service on a committee, one can infer gross characteristics of committee membership that possibly underly the observed tendencies of committees to maintain certain viewpoints. Using the Senate and House Committees on Indian Affairs over a fourteen-year period

(1933 through 1946) as examples, one finds that, regardless of party, the membership of the Committees in both houses was drawn overwhelmingly from Western or Indian-minority-populated states. Over the entire period, among the Democratic members of the Senate Committee, about 90 per cent of the representation was derived from constituencies where Indians were fairly significant minority groups; and for the Republicans the comparable figure was 100 per cent. In the House Committee the comparable figures were 90 per cent and 86 per cent for Democrats and Republicans, respectively. Only half of the states were defined as containing constituencies meeting the above specifications, and these were generally the less densely populated with less than half the total number of Representatives. Therefore, all else equal, the comparable expected figures would have been about 50 per cent in the Senate Committee and even less in the House Committee. In view of their saturation with members elected by white majorities from Indian-minority-populated constituencies, one can better understand the Committees' frequent tendencies to work counter to a Bureau that promoted the interests of Indian minorities in the face of objections by local whites. The same applies for the Committees' greater accessibility to local, non-Indian interest groups. And one is not surprised to find that sectional, ethnic, and socio-economic interests tend to overshadow differences in party label among the members.

On the other hand, the Senate Committee was observed to be more consistent than the House Committee in its hostile activity toward the Bureau's leaders and less inclined toward periodic cooperation with them

in policy development. It has already been suggested
that this was in part a function of greater stability in
Senatorial membership. The committee service figures
tend to lend support and refinement to this conjecture.
The average length of service on the Senate Committee
by Democratic members during this period was 7.3
years, with four of the senior Western Democrats serving throughout the entire fourteen-year period and constituting most of the core or in-group of the Committee.
The average length of service by Republican members
during these New Deal years was 6.2 years, with one
Republican serving the entire fourteen years and being
received generally as a member of the in-group. In the
House Committee no Democrats or Republicans served
for the entire fourteen-year period, and respective average lengths of service were 4.3 and 3.3 years. In general,
one might project the argument that stability of committee membership tends to lend a cohesiveness which
contributes to enduring patterns of behavior in a subsystem.[7]

BEHAVIOR AND INFLUENCE OF APPROPRIATIONS
COMMITTEE PARTICIPANTS

Although substantive committee leaders may maintain the most constant legislative vigilance over and
influence upon a bureau, the crucial leverage of appropriations committees should not be overlooked. The
chairman and key staff members of the subcommittees
on appropriations dealing with a bureau's funds, especially the House subcommittee, have an inside track
on setting a pattern of financial support which may or
may not enable a bureau to carry out policies already

authorized by the Congress. In the years following the passage of the Indian Reorganization Act, Commissioner Collier frequently maintained that major defects in carrying out policy were caused by the failure of Congress to follow through with funds sufficient to execute the plans authorized in the law. The record of appropriations for the Bureau appears to support the general contention that up until the late 1940's at least, the appropriations for economic rehabilitation programs for Indians did not keep pace with either long-term plans or long-term rises in costs.

It seems that at least part of this situation was a consequence of a running battle between Bureau leaders and House Appropriations Subcommittee Chairman Jed Johnson, who reportedly liked to cut every item in the Bureau's appropriation by at least a few dollars in order to maintain a record of frugality. On the other hand, Chairman Johnson made certain that the Bureau would not discontinue an Indian agricultural fair in his home state, even though similar functions elsewhere had been eliminated as a part of wartime economizing. Congressman Johnson so consistently pressed for lower budgets in the Indian Bureau and elsewhere in the Interior Department that finally Secretary Ickes reportedly recommended to the President that Johnson be appointed to a federal judgeship, thereby removing him from his position of influence over the policies of the Department and its bureaus. Before this occurred, however, Johnson and his subcommittee pressed for the resignation of Commissioner Collier after some twelve years in office by threatening to hold up appropriations for the Bureau until Collier left the Commissionership.[8]

BEHAVIOR AND INFLUENCE OF INVESTIGATING
COMMITTEE PARTICIPANTS

Although substantive and appropriations committees do the main share of the legislative work of assigning a bureau its tasks, supplying it with resources, and overseeing the way in which it performs its tasks, certainly the committees whose effects upon public policy are most dramatic and most widely publicized are the investigating units. They come to life and thrive in an atmosphere of extraordinary interest in public good and evil. In recent years the listening and viewing public has come, through radio and television, to know this type of congressional unit better than any other. No doubt the public has formed its images of legislative operations largely on the basis of what it has seen and heard of investigating committees, even though the most publicized ones in many ways have not been typical of congressional committees generally.

Investigating committees and their leaders may vary considerably in the degree of extraordinary publicity they attract and the effects they have upon the course of public policy. Part of this may be attributable to their status in the legislative structure. When an investigating unit is a subcommittee of a standing committee that forcefully exercises control over it and keeps it in line with the views of the members of the larger committee, the subcommittee leaders are less likely to produce sensational or extraordinary effects. Conversely, members of a special investigating committee or a subcommittee which is not restrained by its parental standing committee are freer to pursue their own brand of sensationalism and to have at least some short-run impact upon policy by arousing public sentiment. Another important factor which can affect the nature of an investigation is the relative propensity for restraint or showmanship on the part of the investigating committee chairman, a matter not unrelated to his political aspirations. Still another factor is the length of time an investigating unit has been operating. After a time much of the novelty and excitement may wear off, and the opposition to the investigators may increase and be better mobilized. At that point the main lever of an investigating committee—its atmosphere of Armageddon—may begin to dissipate. If it does not then become more sensational and try to widen its array of targets, the committee is likely to become a routine or ineffective organization, if it does not disband altogether. On the other hand, if it raises its sights on other targets, it may prolong its appeal for a time. Yet, by thus increasing the ranks of its foes, it also increases the likelihood of a more concerted effort by its opposition to end it. Hence, members of investigating committees leaning most heavily upon sensationalism can find themselves the ultimate victims of their own voraciousness when other legislators, the Administration, the mass media, and the public either unite to end them or become tired of their repetitious themes. Investigations, like stage shows, can run out of box-office appeal.

All investigating committees do not necessarily depend upon gross sensationalism to be effective in changing policies in particular areas of our national life, but certainly all depend upon some capacity to penetrate conventional channels of opinion formation and conventional stereotypes. The particular advantages of investigating committees over other types of units accrue largely from whatever privileged access their members are able to obtain both to mass media and to special audiences in positions to "do something about" their findings. These special audiences may be the President, the Attorney General, departmental leaders, or others in positions where they can get the bureau leaders or other subsystem participants to remedy conditions found by the investigation. Another favored type of audience is the grass-roots audience, reached in large measure in the past by staging committee hearings in strategic localities outside of Washington, D. C. In the mid-century era, some committees have combined the touring technique with the advantages of modern communications, especially television and heavy local press and radio coverage, and often the national networks and wire services. The Kefauver Crime Committee, the McCarthy Committee, the McClellan Committee and others have especially exploited these devices. The junketing type of investigation antedated the television era by many decades, but these recent committees demonstrated the possibilities of combining the junket with ultramodern communications techniques. The resulting impact upon the public had never been surpassed. In interpreting the part played by an investigating committee in a subsystem, one must assess its capacity for thus increasing the size of the public interested in a subsystem and for changing the subsystem's relations within the general political structure.

In addition, investigating committees are always potential tools to serve the political ambitions of their leaders and/or the interests of party leaders. To the enterprising and ambitious senator or representative, heading an investigation means getting his name more widely recognized and associated with a fight against some alleged public evil. It offers an opportunity to scale the political ladder at a pace more rapid than a legislator might expect via ordinary channels. This in itself may thrust the affairs of a subsystem into the arena of the two major parties, since the chairman of a strategically placed and timed investigation can constitute a threat both to existing leadership in his own party and also to the balance of power between the parties. At the same time, party leaders may take an interest in the investigation of the affairs of a subsystem commensurate with the opportunities they perceive in it for their political fortunes. The Administration's party may see in it the opportunity to use the power of the investigating committee to bring administrative units and interest groups closer into line with party objectives, something which regular substantive committees may fail to do. The opposition party may see in the investigation the opportunity to exploit defects in bureaucratic performance which will politically embarrass the party in power. Leaders of both parties may join their efforts to control the investigation or to limit it if the investigating committee threatens certain ideas or institutions which they support in common, or if the chairman pushes his public attraction so far that he constitutes a political force threatening the balance of the two-party system.

SOME CONTRASTING EXAMPLES OF INVESTIGATING COMMITTEE STRUCTURES AND EFFECTS

During the Hoover, Roosevelt, and Truman years, several interesting types of investigating committees participated in the political subsystem of Indian affairs. None was as forceful or as dramatic in threatening the equilibrium of the parties, in thrusting the subsystem to the broader political arena, or in projecting the committee chairman into the national spotlight as were the Kefauver, McCarthy, McClellan or similar committees in other areas of public policy. Yet, in a more modest way, some units investigating Indian affairs illustrated points discussed above.

The unit providing the broadest demonstration of varying patterns was the Investigating Subcommittee of the Senate Committee on Indian Affairs. Originally set up in 1928 to "survey the conditions of the Indians of the United States," it lasted for nearly sixteen years. It exemplified the evolution of a committee from initial effectiveness to increasing sensationalism, mistakes, frustration, and eventual demise. The Subcommittee started off under high auspices with the strong backing of many interest groups, as well as of most of the Indians themselves. Its original special counsel was Louis Glavis, well-known as an investigator of Interior Department affairs. When the Subcommittee got under way, the prestigious Brookings Institution was just completing a comprehensive report on changes needed in United States Indian policy. Also, the Hoover Administration, with a new Interior Department team, was soon to assume responsibility in Washington. Although Glavis had to withdraw for physical reasons, the Subcommittee, with a Montana friend of Senator Wheeler's as its new special counsel, proceeded energetically to inquire into many phases of Indian policy and administration. By the end of 1932, after about four years of conducting hearings throughout the country, it had collected two thirds of the total testimony (which finally filled some 23,000 pages) assembled during its entire sixteen years of operations. Many subsequent policies were at least partially based on the evidence brought out in these early years.

After 1932, however, when the New Deal took over, the Senate Subcommittee became more and more a catch basin for complaints and accusations against Collier and the Bureau and less and less a constructive critic. Although the special counsel and the Subcommittee leaders had fairly consistently been opposed from the outset to things which the Bureau of Indian Affairs had done, its opposition seemed to become harsher even as reforms were being instituted in the Bureau.

During its last twelve years this Subcommittee functioned essentially as the inner circle of its parental unit, the Senate Committee on Indian Affairs, often encouraging that unit to listen to groups and individuals who were of the more extreme variety, although markedly diminishing its total collection of testimony. The Senate units especially seemed to afford some of the more favorable forums for representatives of the American Indian Federation—a cluster of small, local groups, held together primarily by highly active and vocal leaders who attempted to pin labels of atheism and communism upon the New Deal program and its officials, while hoping to repeal the Indian Reorganization Act and virtually to abolish the Bureau.

By overreaching its facts and its role, the Subcommittee finally contributed to its own demise. In 1939 and again in 1943 reports against the Bureau of a devastating sort were issued under the label of the Senate Committee, although they had apparently been prepared by Subcommittee staff. Subsequent evidence indicated that the points made in the reports were not fully subscribed to by the Committee leaders who had signed them. In fact, Senator Thomas, Chairman of both the full Committee and the Investigating Subcommittee, found it necessary in 1944 to issue a supplemental report extensively contradicting the 1943 report against the Bureau which only a few months earlier he had signed and issued. Shortly after this incident the sixteen-year-old Investigating Subcommittee was allowed to expire.[9]

The contrast between this Senate Subcommittee and the previously mentioned House Investigating Subcommittee under the direction of Congressman Mundt has already been suggested. Upon its organization in 1944, the latter unit moved to centers of Indian population with alacrity, organized its hearings around major central questions on which the whole Committee had agreed in advance, and submitted a final report which neither completely castigated the Bureau nor was a whitewash, yet which subsequently brought about changes in policy. Then the House Subcommittee disbanded, largely without fanfare or irrelevancy, its members having achieved their purposes within a year. Apparently its members had no stronger political ambitions prodding them than perhaps the normal desires of Western congressmen to go West in an election year, nor did they show any apparent desire to establish a quasi-permanent subcommittee staff. Since they did not present themselves as a unit dedicated to extreme, permanent harassment of the Bureau, they seemed somewhat more capable of getting the cooperation of the Bureau's leaders and of getting their House Subcommittee's views accepted by the Bureau.[10]

In both of the above types of investigatory bodies the

influence of their leaders was circumscribed in varying degrees by the fact that they were still agents of standing Committees on Indian Affairs. They did not constitute intrusions into the subsystem by extraordinary legislative committees from the "outside" political world. In contrast, the Dies Committee on Un-American Activities performed such an intrusion when it furnished an additional forum for the American Indian Federation's charges against Collier, Ickes, and others. Although these charges had previously been made several times in hearings of committees normally concerned with Indian matters, their repetition before the Dies Committee, which reached a larger public, produced a greater reaction within the subsystem.

Subsequently, the measures taken by the Commissioner and by the Secretary of the Interior to counter the charges of the Federation were more intense and more comprehensive. They felt constrained to justify their policies and their personal beliefs for a wider audience, while simultaneously making more extensive efforts to discredit the leaders of the Federation. The Federation's charges were not sustained, but more people had an interest in and opinions about Indian policy, and some no doubt had suspicions emplanted where none had been before. Certainly, the legislators and interest-group leaders who opposed Collier and Ickes gained ammunition for their fight against the New Deal Indian program. Furthermore, much energy and time that might have been used otherwise was expended by the proponents of the New Deal program in holding off the effects of the Dies Committee hearings. Finally, by adding the hearings on the Bureau of Indian Affairs to his committee's string of investigations, Congressman

Dies moved one notch further in his challenge to the general political equilibrium of the period.[11]

COMMITTEE STAFF INFLUENCE

The influence of committee staff members deserves more attention than has been given it in the past, especially in view of the growth in number and in specialization of congressional committee staff personnel in recent years. This growth in committee staffs symbolizes deep sentiments of status-protection in Congress. Underlying a large share of the sometimes-frenetic activities of congressional units toward executive units is the gnawing feeling of legislators that the Administration and the bureaucracy have the advantage in special knowledge, in "inside information," and in man power to be used to confound congressmen and keep them dependent upon the executive branch. A major remedy, as committee members see it, is to have staff personnel of their own who can in some measure redress the balance and help restore independence and higher status to the legislative units. To some extent this does appear to be the result of the fuller staffing of committees that has occurred in recent years. Certainly, larger and more qualified staffs furnish committee leaders with information apart from the reports of the bureaucracy. They are also agents whose loyalties are more likely to lie in the direction of committee leaders. Yet, in another sense, increased committee staffing does not eliminate the dependency of committee members upon others for information, but only transfers it from bureaucrats to committee staff experts. The sources of a congressman's dependency upon some kinds of specialists lie considerably beyond the need for committee staff help; they lie in the many competing demands upon legislators' time and in the complex variety of issues which they must attempt to resolve. Consequently, well-entrenched, well-trained, and astute committee staff members are often in quite favorable positions to be "powers behind the scenes" insofar as committee members transfer their dependency to them.

The chief staff members of committees today are usually sufficiently well-trained and sufficiently cloaked with experience and with the privileges and protections of the Congress to enable them to be quite effective in shaping the course of committee decisions. They do much of the real work of the committees, a great deal of which may be quite remote from public scrutiny. They usually determine the agenda of committee hearings and screen the information which comes into committee records with considerable finality. They draft committee reports and recommendations, and by the subtle processes of inclusion and exclusion can structure the alternatives upon which final committee votes are taken. Furthermore, in their roles as agents of committees they can make special investigations of bureau policies and organization through which they can inject their views into the affairs of bureaus beyond the limits that their formal positions would imply. More than one ranking committee staff member has been regarded by bureau officials as the bête noire on Capitol Hill.

SOME BASIC FACTORS IN COMMITTEE MEMBERS' RECEPTIVITY TO POLICY VIEWPOINTS

We have already indicated some of the conditions related to the fact that committee leaders and members may act and think differently from bureau leaders about issues in the subsystem. One factor is the nature of the legislative role, in which committee members are supposed to choose wisely among policy alternatives of a complex sort and simultaneously protect interests of their constituents, all the while being urged to accede to the bureaucrats' greater technical knowledge. Another factor is the greater proximity of the legislator to a local social setting which he not only represents as spokesman but of which he is usually a representative product. Still another factor is a common desire to protect the status of legislators vis-à-vis bureaucrats, and further, to be champion of the citizen with a complaint against the labyrinths of bureaucratic procedures. Related to this is a frequent preference for information from sources which are "non-executive" in nature, information from committee staff, from the grass-roots, from unhappy bureau employees, or sometimes from leaders of bureaus that have clearly cast their lot with Congress.

Consequently, committee members do not uniformly sit back and hear a bureau's case and then decide the issue on what, from the bureau leaders' perspectives, would be called the merits. Despite their demand that bureaus keep them informed, committee members are frequently suspicious of the information that bureaus give them. Moreover, they frequently feel that it is their duty to promote views counter to those of a bureau's spokesmen. That they do this does not necessarily justify the inference that committee members are either unenlightened or malicious, although bureau leaders who have received such treatment often believe this to be true. It may be that some committee members do not define the situation, the issues, or the standards by which to judge information in the same light as the bureaucrats.

When the leaders of the Bureau of Indian Affairs came before the Committees on Indian Affairs, committee members often viewed them as representatives of a power center seeking to enhance their own power and that of their superiors as well as the security of their subordinates. Sometimes they were also regarded as a power center challenging the committee members for the loyalty of their Indian constituents. Their arguments were regarded as rationalizations of their interests. The principles underlying their arguments were deemed to be theories which did not encompass the range of facts asserted to be most relevant by some of the committee members. Extension of protection of Indian property was often regarded as an excuse for prolonging the life of the Bureau and for keeping Indians from being "emancipated." By this light, personnel of the Bureau became "theorists" who knew too little at first hand about either Indians or the law. Reflected in the frames of reference of some committee members were those ancient criteria of practical knowledge and ability, whereby bureaucratic attorneys are deemed impractical if they have "never tried a case," and public servants are written off if they have "neither carried a precinct nor met a payroll." Considerable time was spent in trying to show that the Commissioner could not know as much about the needs of Indians in the various states as did the legislators from those states. Opportunities were often sought to discredit lawyers and witnesses for the Bureau's side, and many assists were given to witnesses taking opposing points of view.

Congressman Theodore B. Werner, in the course of a House Committee hearing, used a phrase that is in some ways a happy one for emphasizing the importance of differences in bureaucratic and legislative perspective. Werner complained that newspaper writers had maligned traveling investigations as "junkets." The Congressman protested that this was not the case at all, but that traveling committee hearings were most essential ways of getting "informative information." Judging on the basis of his reactions and those of others on both the House and Senate Committees, a great deal of the information from the Bureau and its friends was not viewed as "informative." Instead of hearing from bureaucrats whose livelihood depended upon the Bureau, or interest-group leaders from the East who did not face Indian problems at first hand and who were long-time associates of the Commissioner's, or from "Bureau Indians," or from anthropologists who were interested in preserving Indian culture, many committee members preferred to go West to talk with the Indians' and whites whom they knew best and who thought as they did.[12] This was, to some committee members, "informative information." Of course, it may not have differed in its basic nature from that kind of information for which most mortals have a preference. For the psychologists tell us that we tend to perceive situations in accordance with expectations built up through long-time conditioning.

THE EBB AND FLOW OF GROUP EFFECTIVENESS IN THE SUBSYSTEM

Men have long speculated about the tides of politics. Various observations have been made of long-term trends in political affairs indicating the cyclical nature of patterns of power. But an understanding of the exact nature and the causes of these possible "cycles" is far from being at a stage of definitive theoretical or empirical demonstration. Be that as it may, it is worthwhile to consider the possibility that in subsystems the influence of groups expressing certain orientations waxes and wanes and shifts its focus from one part of the subsystem to another, although not necessarily in neat, evenly spaced cycles. At the risk of considerable oversimplification, some general patterns and crucial factors in the ebb and flow of group alignments and influence in Indian affairs will be attempted below.

Among the publics of Indian affairs there have been three major points of view in the period since 1928, and the groups holding them have been fairly consistent, although they shifted, combined, and reorganized from time to time. There were the so-called protectionists, composed largely of members of secular welfare associations of a cosmopolitan sort, with many Easterners in their number. Also, groups of Indians were increasingly organized and affiliated with the protectionist point of view, which advocated a strong federal program of Indian services and assistance as well as freedom for Indians to choose whether they wanted federal wardship over them to continue. The second viewpoint was that of a group known as the moderates, typified by certain sectarian welfare groups, by missionaries, and other Indian sympathizers of both the East and West. Although they were generally for the protection of Indians, they also were more inclined to push them toward the white man's way of living than would the protectionists. Finally, there were the anti-protectionists, predominantly local, Western groups, some of whom were the more nearly assimilated Indians. Generally, they advocated an end to federal wardship and services, claiming that the Indians wanted "emancipation" and should stand on their own feet. During the last thirty-five years the dominant pattern of effort and effectiveness by groups representing these viewpoints has been as follows: (1) The protectionists have tended more often to support the Bureau, usually working to mobilize the clientele to help keep the Bureau in line with their objectives. (2) The moderates, as might be expected, have been less consistently aligned with either the Bureau or the Committees, tending to support and be effective in the Bureau in periods of transition from one extreme in policy to the other and playing a less effective part in the periods of extreme alignment of forces. (3) The anti-protectionists have fairly consistently aligned themselves with the Committees and have usually been more effective there, capitalizing upon the tendencies of many members to reflect the sentiments of their Western constituents against protection of Indians.

However, observations based on a comparatively short time span leave out of consideration possible long-term trends in general political sentiment. There is some probability that over longer periods covering major shifts in public outlook and political power, other patterns would be observed. For instance, it is also true that over the long run a chief characteristic of the Committees has been to serve as a sounding board for those interests which have the greatest difficulty influencing the Bureau directly. Thus, despite considerable sympathy among many members of the Committees with the anti-protectionists' views (since they are generally closer to the views of most Western legislators and their non-Indian constituents), in periods of extreme anti-protectionism in the Bureau the Committees may begin to give audience to the protectionists. In fact, this apparently was the case in 1928 and even earlier, when Collier and other protectionists worked with the Committees against a Bureau that had been very lax in protecting Indian rights during the Harding and Coolidge Administrations. The legislators attacked the Bureau even though many members of the Committee probably did not agree with Collier on the degree of protection necessary for Indians. Over the long run the tendencies toward extremes in policy thus seemed to be modified as the "outs" used the Committees to work against the dominant point of view espoused by the Bureau.

CHAPTER SIX

✿ ✿ ✿

The Subsystem
in Perspective

✿ ✿ ✿

A SUMMARY JUSTIFICATION OF THE STUDY'S FOCUS

In focusing upon the relations among executive bureau participants, congressional committee personnel, and leaders of interest groups in subsystems of public policy-making in American government, this study has attempted to demonstrate a useful way of examining the political process. It has argued for the utility of this kind of analytical approach partially upon the basis that the study of national policy-making at the more general, institutional level of Congress, the Administration, and the political parties does not always furnish the most meaningful understanding of the decisive factors. The case has been argued that the social diversity, the multiplicity of types of special groups of people promoting and defending particular values in American life, results in selective concentration of public interest and attention in politics. Concomitantly, the legislative and executive branches of the federal government cloak plural patterns of power and decision-making which mirror the functional specialization and diversity of interests in the society to a great extent. Furthermore, the legal framework in which this overall governmental system is cast contributes a permissive code not only making for a maximum of interplay between the legislative and executive branches in policy-making, but also allowing considerable decentralization of authority within each branch.

Consequently, we find that the overall, institutional system which forms the general setting for the executive bureau–legislative committee subsystem tends to have definite limitations as a decisive policy-making mechanism. While the Administration, Congress, and the major parties in their general structures and relationships tend to reflect gross distribution of public sentiment and public power, the resolution of issues tends to be accomplished through specialized lesser units. These subunits—bureaus, committees, and interest groups—enjoy considerable autonomy in the special policy areas with which they are concerned. Furthermore, these are the units which provide the immediate setting of the subsystem here under analysis. The leading members of these subunits are the major, constant participants in a process through which special issues are discussed and policy solutions are formed. In their interactions which form the subsystem, the behavior of the participants is most immediately affected by the nature and interests of the subunits which they lead.

The patterns of interaction in the subsystem are, of course, not by any means completely beyond the pale of influence of the leaders of the Administration, of Congress, or of the political parties. The nature and also the limitations of top-level influence, however, were seen to be such that, except under rather unusual and optimum conditions, the subsystem is likely to be sufficiently decisive so as to warrant an orderly and detailed examination of the relations within it.

SOME PROPOSITIONS ABOUT THE SUBSYSTEM

The major types of strategy and means of influence of the participants in the subsystem will be summarized here as a conclusion to the study.

SUMMARY PROPOSITIONS REGARDING THE BUREAU LEADERS IN THE SUBSYSTEM

Crucial to the bureau leader's objective of obtaining favorable responses from committee members to his policy proposals is his *strategic sensitivity*, or his ability to recognize and to anticipate the expectations of committee members and to relate this to his own actions. Of course, a critical part of this strategic sensitivity lies in recognizing the interests of powerful committee members and making the necessary accommodations.

In attempting to influence committee members, the bureau leader has numerous direct and indirect means at his disposal. *One alternative is the exploitation of high-level power and prestige symbols by using the support of dominant figures in the Administration.* This strategy is most likely to be employed where there are strong and mutually reinforcing bonds of an interest or ideological nature (or both) between the bureau leader and the higher echelon figures. The strategy is most likely to have an effect upon the committee members when the general public acclaim and support for the Administration is so overwhelming as to offset possible negative reactions which committee members might develop against the bureau leader's use of such pressures. Furthermore, even though this strategy may maximize the influence of the bureaucrat in the subsystem, it is also likely to enlarge the area of controversy in which he and his organization become involved.

Increasingly, attempts of bureau leaders to influence committee members are being routinized through provision in the departmental organizational structure for specialists in legislative liaison. This organized legislative liaison is most important as a communications device on day-to-day matters and for dealing with the extensive number of routine requests from legislators. Its cumulative effect, however, is an important conditioner of the official's relations with committee members, and key individuals in the legislative liaison set-up may be important adjuncts to the bureau leader's efforts.

Personal friendship or other personal sentiments between a bureau leader and key committee members can also be crucial elements in his ability to gain favorable responses from the committees. The oversimplified use of personality factors to explain a bureau leader's success or failure along this line nevertheless probably should be avoided. It is sometimes too simple and easy just to attribute the consequences to the compatibility or incompatibility of certain personalities. *The chances are that personal relationships of a favorable type may be as frequently disrupted by the diverse roles which bureaucrat and legislative committeemen have to play as the other way around.* Furthermore, while length of tenure of office may give a bureaucrat time to develop favorable personal relationships in a committee, there is no assurance that the obverse may not also occur in which once-favorable personal relationships deteriorate over the years under the conflicting demands of bureaucratic and legislative roles and conflicting interests.

Still further, *what holds true for a bureau leader's personal relations with committee members can hold true also in his relations with group leaders who may support or oppose his proposals before the committees.* In his relations with group leaders, however, the bureau leader may maintain the support of some by institutionalizing his friendship with them by appointing them to official posts in the bureau. On the other hand, such action is likely to be regarded as favoritism by group leaders not thus honored, thereby increasing their efforts against the bureau leader's objectives.

Although committee hearings are manifestly means for the rational communication of factual information, often the exploitation of the non-rational aspects of committee hearings is more important to the type and degree of response which the bureau leader elicits than are the facts which he presents. This means, on the one hand, that his influence with the committee may depend not so much upon what he says as upon the impression the committee members form of him as a communicator and as a bureaucrat. On the other hand, it also means that the skill with which a bureau leader is able to exploit the supposed public impact of his testimony in the minds of the committee members will be closely related to his ability to influence them.

In the use of publicity and propaganda, the bureau leader may capitalize upon two conditions to influence the course of decision in the subsystem. First, the interested publics of the subsystem are usually sufficiently restricted in size so that extensive propaganda campaigns are not ordinarily necessary to reach the critical audience. Second, because the inside or trade media are likely to reach the most interested publics, the bureau leader by virtue of his status may not only enjoy ready access to most of the nonofficial trade channels but also has the advantage of controlling the official media emanating from the bureau. Nevertheless, undue exploitation of either type may generate adverse reactions in the long run by violating the committee members' conceptions of the proper publicity role for bureaucrats.

A bureau leader generally finds it necessary to have at least the support of most of the bureau's employees and most of its clientele in order to assert his policy views successfully before committee members. Such support is likely to be one of the minimum conditions for committee acceptance of his policy proposals. This is not as easily accomplished as one might think at first glance, since employee and clientele groups are not cohesive units in most instances. Furthermore, besides a tendency to resist too much pressure from the bureau leadership, these groups usually show considerable propensity for internal schisms in which the bureau leaders often alienate one faction in the attempt to win the affections of another. If bureau leaders can mobilize the support of employees and clientele in the home territories of committee members, the consequences in the short run may be quite helpful in getting committee acceptance of proposed policies, especially if committee members are consulted in the process. Over the long run, however, such action runs the risk of involving the bureau leadership in the political affairs of committee members' constituents, which may very likely produce results adverse to the objectives of the bureaucrats. Local reaction may develop against the use of this strategy by bureau officials, and local interests may consolidate against them.

In mobilizing support among non-internal groups, bureau leaders are more likely to find initial sympathy among those segments of the public which are interested in the clientele, though not a part of it, which are less local and more cosmopolitan in their orientations, and which are more prone to be concerned with the bureau's policies on ideological grounds rather than material interests. The ability of such groups to influence committee members, however, is often not as great as that of the locally-based groups who frequently have the advantage in working through those constituents of committee members who are not clients of the bureau.

By admitting members of certain groups to the policy-making councils of the bureau, either through consultation or by official appointment, bureau leaders can often maximize the support of such groups in behalf of the bureau before the committees. Conversely, leaders and members of groups not thus coopted may tend to be the most vociferous opponents of the bureau leaders and may serve as strong counterforces to the acceptance of their proposals by committee members.

SUMMARY PROPOSITIONS REGARDING COMMITTEE PARTICIPANTS IN THE SUBSYSTEM

By exploiting the broad sanctions which are available to them, committee participants can wield great influence in the subsystem, both in determining the content of legislation and in shaping its administration. The three major types of committee sanctions are approval or disapproval of substantive legislation, approval or disapproval of appropriations, and investigation of subsystem affairs.

The substantive committee leaders tend to constitute the most constant congressional influentials in subsystem policy-making. They are frequently able to exercise a major degree of censorship over the final legislative product; especially, is this true of the veteran members of the committee in-group. They are likely to be the most powerful and most concerned members of Congress in a given policy area. Their interests become major factors in the process.

Substantive committees frequently attract a predominance of members with particular social backgrounds and characteristics. The major enduring social characteristics in such cases help in understanding the members' behavior in policy-making over the long run insofar as that behavior tends to reflect value patterns of the subcultures in which the members have achieved political success. *The predominance of one major set of subcultural values among the members of a committee will tend to lend a consistent pattern to their policy-making activities which transcends such factors as partisan differences.*

Also, *length of service of committee members pro-*

duces a degree of stability in committee membership patterns, lending a cohesiveness which is reflected in the members' behavior. The longer average tenure of senators may be relevant to a greater constancy in the reactions of Senate committee members to bureau leaders' proposals in comparison to the reactions of House committee members.

Though legislative committee members are perhaps the most constant influentials on the legislative side of the subsystem and though they may ultimately give the bureau leaders much of what they desire in the way of authorized policies, the members of the appropriations committees possess what is probably the strongest single sanction and may effectively negate authorized policies and force administrative changes by refusing the necessary resources. Here the decisive part tends to be played by leaders of the subcommittees on appropriations who are the real specialists in the financial affairs of particular bureaus. Especially is this true of the chairman of a given House appropriations subcommittee. His function is frequently that of basic arbiter over the allocation of financial resources for a bureau, a power which he may use to accomplish ends well beyond the overt objectives of the appropriations process. As a general rule, the strongest pressures for cutting a bureau's funds emanate from members of the House appropriations subcommittee, who are by custom the first and closest legislative scrutinizers of the budget proposals. Senate appropriations subcommittee members tend to concern themselves with questions of whether to restore cuts made in the House.

Investigating committee participants in the subsystem vary in their influence to a considerable degree in ac-

*cordance with their ability to break through settled
channels of opinion formation and conventional stereotypes about issues among public groups.* They tend to
increase in impact as they enlarge the public interested
in the subsystem. Over the long run, however, members
of investigating committees which have exploited the
potentialities for sensationalism to the utmost and have
consistently widened the targets of their operations are
likely to reach a point of diminishing effect. This may
be due to the accumulation of opposition which is
likely to crystallize eventually in an effort to halt the
investigation or may result from eventual public weari-
ness with the committee's repetitive theme. Furthermore, where the investigation is used as an adjunct to
the political hopes of the committee leader, the leaders
of one or both of the major parties may intervene in the
subsystem in an effort to protect the balance of power
in the party system.

*Due to demands upon committee members' time,
knowledge, and attention, their dependency upon others
for information, judgment, and executive action contributes to the influential roles played by committee
staff.* High-ranking, long-time committee staff members
tend to control the communications channels of committees, draft committee reports, and as committee
agents may inject their views into the subsystem in ways
and to degrees that their formal roles might not imply.

*The committee member's role, in which he is ex-
pected to choose wisely among policy alternatives as
well as to represent his local constituency, tends to create blocks against his receptivity to the views of bureau
 ·ders, despite their often-alleged superior technical
. Frequently, the committee member feels a

strong urge to protect his status as the lawmaker in the face of bureaucratic challenge. Consequently, the committee member often prefers information and suggestions about policy from sources other than bureau leaders and their allies. Furthermore, he may often play something less than a neutral role in the deliberations within the subsystem by giving encouragement to non-bureau spokesmen. Certainly, even if the committee member does not feel especially sensitive about his status relative to that of bureaucrats, on occasions in which the committee member's interests lie counter to the bureau leader's, he may find it convenient to pretend that the bureaucrat is attempting to pre-empt the legislative function and to lay claim to a superiority of knowledge that is based on theory rather than on practicality.

The influence and effectiveness of groups in a subsystem may well follow long-range cyclical patterns. Over a period of more than a decade, during which the bureau leadership and the supporting leadership of the Administration were both unchanged, the pattern of group alignments for and against the policies of the bureau leaders remained fairly constant. But this was in one subsystem during an exceptionally long continuity in the policy orientation of the bureau. On the basis of a wider observation of the patterns of group-leader intervention in the subsystem, the broadest pattern appeared likely to be that tendencies toward extremes in policy were modified by a process in which the "outs" used the committee members as sounding boards to work against the bureau leaders and their associated group leaders.

Notes
to the Study

CHAPTER ONE

1. Griffith, Ernest S.: *The Impasse of Democracy* (New York, Harrison-Hilton Books, Inc., 1939), p. 182. Quoted in Griffith, Ernest S.: *Congress: Its Contemporary Role* (3rd ed.; New York, New York University Press, 1961), pp. 50-51.

2. Cater, Douglass: *Power in Washington* (New York, Random House, 1964), esp. Chaps. I, II, and XIV.

3. In addition to Cater's book cited above, one may find particularly helpful on this subject Hyneman, Charles S.: *Bureaucracy in a Democracy* (New York, Harper & Brothers, 1950), Chaps. V, XI, and XXI; also Woll, Peter: *American Bureaucracy* (New York, W. W. Norton & Co., 1963).

4. Bentley, Arthur F.: *The Process of Government* (Chicago, University of Chicago Press, 1908).

5. Wallas, Graham: *Human Nature in Politics* (Lincoln, University of Nebraska Press, 1908).

6. Herring, E. Pendleton: *Group Representation before Congress* (Baltimore, The Johns Hopkins Press, 1929); also, Herring: *Public Administration and the Public Interest* (New York, McGraw-Hill Book Co., 1936).

7. Truman, David B.: *The Governmental Process* (New York, Knopf, 1951).

8. Key, V. O., Jr.: "Legislative Control," in Morstein-Marx, Fritz (ed.), *Elements of Public Administration* (New York, Prentice-Hall, Inc., 1946); Key, V. O., Jr.: *Politics, Parties and Pressure Groups* (5th ed.; New York, Thomas Y. Crowell Co., 1964), Chap. XXV.

9. Leiserson, Avery: *Administrative Regulation: A Study in Representation of Interests* (Chicago, University of Chicago Press, 1942).

10. Wilson, Woodrow: *Congressional Government* (Boston, Houghton Mifflin Co., 1885).

11. For example: Young, Roland: *This is Congress* (New York, Knopf, 1943); and Young: *The American Congress* (New York, Harper & Row, 1958); Galloway, George B.: *Congress at the Crossroads* (New York, Thomas Y. Crowell Co., 1946); also, Galloway: *The Legislative Process in Congress* (New York, Thomas Y. Crowell Co., 1953); Kefauver, Estes and Levin, Jack: *A Twentieth Century Congress* (New York, Duell, ...n, and Pearce, 1947); Burns, James M.: *Con-*

gress on Trial (New York, Harper & Row, 1949); Griffith: *Congress: Its Contemporary Role, op. cit.*; White, William S.: *Citadel: The Story of the U. S. Senate* (New York, Harper & Row, 1956); Acheson, Dean: *A Citizen Looks at Congress* (New York, Harper & Row, 1957); MacNeil, Neil: *Forge of Democracy: The House of Representatives* (New York, David McKay Co., Inc., 1963); Thomas, Norman C. and Lamb, Karl A.: *Congress: Politics and Practice* (New York, Random House, 1964); Clark, Joseph S.: *Congress: The Sapless Branch* (New York, Harper & Row, 1964). The most recent survey of literature ranging widely over this field is provided in the excellent work by Keefe, William J. and Ogul, Morris S.: *The American Legislative Process: Congress and the States* (New York, Prentice-Hall, 1964).

12. Some varied examples: Gross, Bertram: *The Legislative Struggle: A Study in Social Combat* (New York, McGraw-Hill Book Co., 1953); Matthews, Donald R.: *U. S. Senators and Their World* (Chapel Hill, University of North Carolina Press, 1960); also, Matthews: *The Social Background of Political Decision Makers* (New York, Random House, 1954); Clapp, Charles L.: *The Congressman: His Work as He Sees It* (Washington, The Brookings Institution, 1963); and though based on state legislatures, the most exacting study of comparative legislative behavior is Wahlke, John C., Eulau, Heinz, Buchanan, William, and Ferguson, LeRoy: *The Legislative System: Explorations in Legislative*

Behavior (New York, John Wiley & Sons, Inc., 1962).

13. For example: Chamberlain, Lawrence: *The President, Congress, and Legislation* (New York, Columbia University Press, 1946); Binkley, Wilfred E.: *President and Congress* (New York, Knopf, 1947), also, Vintage Books, 1962; Fenno, Richard: *The President's Cabinet* (Cambridge, Harvard University Press, 1959); and the works of Hyneman and of Woll, previously cited; also Burns, James M.: *The Deadlock of Democracy* (New York, Prentice-Hall, 1963).

14. Harris, Joseph P.: *Congressional Control of Administration* (Washington, The Brookings Institution, 1964).

15. Blaisdell, Donald C.: *American Democracy Under Pressure* (New York, The Ronald Press Co., 1957); Milbrath, Lester W.: *The Washington Lobbyists* (Chicago, Rand McNally & Co., 1963); Zeigler, Harmon: *Interest Groups in American Society* (New York, Prentice-Hall, 1964); also, "Unofficial Government: Pressure Groups and Lobbies," *The Annals*, Vol. 319 (Sept., 1958) (edited by Donald C. Blaisdell).

16. Latham, Earl: *The Group Basis of Politics* (Ithaca, N. Y., Cornell University Press, 1952); Bailey, Stephen K.: *Congress Makes a Law* (New York, Columbia University Press, 1950); Riggs, Fred W.: *Pressures on Congress* (New York, King's Crown Press, Columbia University, 1950); among the newer ones are Witte, Edwin E.: *The Development of the Social Security Act* (Madison, University of Wisconsin Press, 1962);

Wildavsky, Aaron: *Dixon-Yates: A Study in Power Politics* (New Haven, Yale University Press, 1962); Berman, Daniel A.: *A Bill Becomes a Law: The Civil Rights Act of 1960* (New York, The Macmillan Co., 1962).

17. Maass, Arthur A.: *Muddy Waters* (Cambridge, Harvard University Press, 1951); Hardin, Charles M.: *The Politics of Agriculture* (Glencoe, Ill., The Free Press, 1952); Huzar, Elias: *The Purse and the Sword* (Ithaca, N. Y., Cornell University Press, 1950); among newer ones are Wengert, Norman C.: *Natural Resources and the Political Struggle* (New York, Random House, 1961); Foss, Philip O.: *Politics and Grass: The Administration of Grazing in the Public Domain* (Seattle, University of Washington Press, 1960); Robinson, James A.: *Congress and Foreign Policy Making* (Homewood, Ill., The Dorsey Press, 1962).

CHAPTER TWO

1. For other statements on this topic, see especially Griffith: *Congress: Its Contemporary Role, op. cit.*, pp. 7, 109-23. See also Wilson, Woodrow: *Constitutional Government in the United States* (New York, Columbia University Press, 1908), pp. 56-57; Key: *Politics, Parties, and Pressure Groups, op. cit.*, pp. 691-705.

2. Committee on Political Parties of the American Political Science Association: *Toward a More Responsible Two-Party System*, supplement to the *American Political Science Review*, Vol. 44, No. 3 (Sept., 1950); Schattschneider, E. E.:

Party Government (New York, Farrar and Rinehart, Inc., 1942); Truman: *The Governmental Process, op. cit.,* pp. 270-87.

3. Key: *Politics, Parties, and Pressure Groups, op. cit.,* pp. 329-44.

4. Burns: *The Deadlock of Democracy, op. cit.*

5. For examples of various reform proposals for the legislative and executive branches as well as for the party system, see Elliot, W. Y.: *The Need for Constitutional Reform* (New York, Whittlesey House, 1935); Corwin, Edward S.: *The President: Office and Powers* (3rd ed.; New York, New York University Press, 1948); Hyneman: *Bureaucracy in a Democracy, op. cit.;* U. S. President's Committee on Administrative Management: *Report of the President's Committee* (Washington, D. C., Government Printing Office, 1937); U. S. Commission on Organization of the Executive Branch of the Government: *General Management of the Executive Branch* (Washington, D. C., Government Printing Office, 1949); Committee on Political Parties of the American Political Science Association, *loc. cit.*

6. In the period since World War II, some of the "fulcrum" function of bureau chiefs has been passed upward to assistant secretaries, perhaps. But the basic pattern is still there. In 1954, articles were being written, e.g., concerning the problems of coordinated policy-making in the State Department. Ten years later, the Secretary of State was complaining of problems of "layering," of being far removed from actual confronta-

tion with his agency's work, due to layers of subordinates. See Collins, Frederic W.: "New Tests for 'State,'" *The New York Times Magazine* (May 23, 1954), pp. 8-9; and Briggs, Ellis O.: "Case Against a West Point for Diplomats," *The New York Times Magazine* (May 3, 1964), pp. 20 ff.

7. Cater: *op. cit.*, Chap IX.
8. Clark: *Congress: The Sapless Branch, op. cit.*, pp. 137-39.
9. *Ibid.*, Chap. VI.
10. Wilson: *Congressional Government, op. cit.*
11. Wilson: *Constitutional Government, op. cit.*, p. 92.
12. David Riesman in *The Lonely Crowd* (New Haven, Yale University Press, 1950) speaks of these groups as primarily veto groups. Although much of their effort is defensive, this term is inadequate for the roles which they play within limited arenas of policy-making. There they take the offense, while outside their special domains of effective action they do not always have the complete defensive power which the term veto implies. See also the comments in Latham: *The Group Basis of Politics, op. cit.*, pp. 36-37.

CHAPTER THREE

1. See, for example, Burnham, James: *Congress and the American Tradition* (Chicago, Henry Regnery Co., 1959); or most any issue of *The National Review*.

2. Neustadt, Richard: *Presidential Power: The Politics of Leadership* (New York, John Wiley & Sons, Inc., 1960), p. 5.

3. Discussions of the role of the Bureau of the Budget are to be found in Morstein-Marx, Fritz: "The Bureau of the Budget: Its Evolution and Present Role," *American Political Science Review* 39:653-84, 869-98 (August and October, 1945); Key: "Legislative Control," in Morstein-Marx (ed.), *Elements of Public Administration, op. cit.*, pp. 350-51; Truman: *op. cit.*, pp. 428-30; Maass, Arthur: "In Accord with the Program of the President?" in Friedrich, C. J. and J. K. Galbraith (eds.), *Public Policy* (Cambridge, Graduate School of Public Administration, Harvard University, 1953), pp. 77-93.

4. President Kennedy's first order of business after his election was to state his intention to reappoint Mr. Hoover. See Cater: *op. cit.*, p. 10. Subsequently, in 1964 under President Johnson, Mr. Hoover was allowed to extend his service beyond the usual retirement age of seventy.

5. The two laws in question are: 38 Stat. L. 212 and 41 Stat. L. 68. See McCamy, James L.: *Government Publicity* (Chicago, University of Chicago Press, 1939), for a full analysis of this subject.

6. See McCamy: *op. cit.*; Stoke, Harold: "Executive Leadership and the Growth of Propaganda," *American Political Science Review* 35:490-500 (June, 1941); House Select Committee on Lobbying Activities: *Legislative Activities of Executive Agencies*, Washington, D. C., Government Printing Office, 1950, Pt. 10 of Hearings on H.

Res. 298, 81st Cong., 2nd Sess.; Witte, Edwin
E.: "Administrative Agencies and Statute Law-
making," *Public Administration Review* 2:116 ff.
(Spring, 1942).

7. Neustadt: *op. cit.*, Chaps. I & II.

8. Shanahan, Eileen: "Saxon Gets the Word: Stay
in Line," *New York Times*, March 22, 1964.

9. U. S. Congress, Senate. Committee on Indian
Affairs. *Survey of Conditions of the Indians in
the United States*. Hearings pursuant to S. Res.
79, 70th Cong., 2nd Sess. and subsequent continuing resolutions (Washington, Government
Printing Office, 1938), Pt. 37.

10. Maass: *Muddy Waters, op. cit.*

11. For an analysis of the various theories of representative government, see DeGrazia, Alfred:
Public and Republic (New York, Knopf, 1951).

12. Keefe and Ogul: *op. cit.*, pp. 238-44.

13. Further views on the effects of the Legislative
Reorganization Act of 1946 are to be found in
Thomas, Elbert D.: "How Congress Functions
Under Its Reorganization Act," *American Politi-
cal Science Review* 43:1179-88 (December,
1949); Galloway, George B.: "The Operations
of the Legislative Reorganization Act of 1946,"
American Political Science Review 45:41-68
(March, 1951).

14. House Select Committee on Lobbying Activities:
American Enterprise Association (Washington,
D. C., Government Printing Office, 1950), H.
Report 3233, 81st Cong., 2nd Sess.

15. Taken in part from televised press interview with
Senator Guy M. Gillette (Dem.-Iowa) on "Meet

the Press," NBC, May 30, 1954. See also Wilson, H. Hubert: *Congress: Corruption and Compromise* (New York, Rinehart & Co., 1951); and White, William S.: "The 'Club' that is the U. S. Senate," *The New York Times Magazine*, November 7, 1954, pp. 9 ff. The Bobby Baker inquiry ten years after the McCarthy censure seemed to indicate a continuing tendency in the Senate toward treading lightly upon hallowed ground.

16. Galloway: *op. cit.*, p. 46, points out that as of the end of 1950 the Atomic Energy Committee was the only joint committee with actual legislative powers, while the Joint Committee on the Economic Report was the next most important, though without legislative teeth.

17. Huzar: *The Purse and the Sword*, *op. cit.*, pp. 36-39, 76.

18. See *The New York Times*, July 18, 1954, p. 25.

19. *New York Times*, June 28, 1964, p. 1.

20. *St. Paul Pioneer Press*, April 5, 1950, and *Minneapolis Tribune*, same date; quoted in House Select Committee on Lobbying Activities, *op. cit.*, Hearings, Pt. 10, pp. 248-250.

21. White, William S.: "The Pressures That Drive a Congressman," *The New York Times Magazine*, June 6, 1954, p. 9 ff.

CHAPTER FOUR

1. Freeman, J. L., Jr.: "The New Deal for Indians: A Study in Bureau–Committee Relations in

American Government." Unpublished doctoral dissertation, Princeton University, 1952.

2. For references to some of these studies see the works cited in footnotes 5 and 6, Chap. I.

3. Cater: *op. cit.*, Chaps. I & II.

4. Ickes, Harold L.: *The Secret Diary of Harold L. Ickes: The First Thousand Days, 1933-1936* (New York, Simon and Schuster, 1953), p. 360 especially.

5. Senate Committee on Indian Affairs, Hearings on S. 2755 (Washington, D. C., Government Printing Office, 1934), 73rd Cong., 2nd Sess., Pt. 1, pp. 85-86.

6. *Ibid.*, p. 86. Italics the author's.

7. *Ibid.*, p. 23.

8. House Committee on Indian Affairs, Subcommittee Hearings on H. R. 7781 (Washington, D. C., Government Printing Office, 1935), 74th Cong., 1st Sess., p. 728.

9. Freeman: *op. cit.*, Chaps. VI and VII.

10. *Ibid.*, Chap. VIII.

11. See Johnson, Earl D.: "Legislative–Executive Relationships in the Formulation of Public Policy as Viewed by the Executive," in *Legislative–Executive Relationships in the Government of the United States* (Washington, D. C., U. S. Department of Agriculture Graduate School, 1954), pp. 26-34.

12. Freeman: *op. cit.*, Chaps. II, IV, and V especially.

13. *Ibid.*, pp. 401-412.

14. For a suggestive study of relations between officials and reporters, see Nimmo, Dan D., *News-*

gathering in Washington (New York, Atherton Press, 1962).

15. Freeman: *op. cit.*, Chaps. III, IV, and VI.

CHAPTER FIVE

1. Freeman, *op. cit.*, Chaps. IV, V, VI, and VIII.
2. Selznick, Philip: *TVA and the Grass Roots* (Berkeley and Los Angeles, University of California Press, 1949).
3. Harris: *Congressional Control of Administration, op. cit.*
4. Keefe and Ogul: *The American Legislative Process, op. cit.*
5. Woll: *American Bureaucracy, op. cit.*
6. Freeman: *op. cit.*, Chap. IV.
7. *Ibid.*, Chap. I.
8. *Ibid.*, Chap. VII.
9. *Ibid.*, Chaps. II and VI.
10. *Ibid.*, pp. 401-412.
11. *Ibid.*, pp. 381-386.
12. *Ibid.*, Chap. III.

Index

Administrative decentraliza-
tion, 23-4
AFL-CIO, 56, 58, 60
Agriculture Department, 89
Aiken, George D., 60
American Enterprise Associa-
tion, 50
American Indian Defense As-
sociation, 79, 86
American Indian Federation,
108, 110
Appropriations Committees,
52, 80-1, 101-2
influence on subsystem, 101-
2
Ashurst, Henry F., 98
Association on American In-
dian Affairs, 86

Bentley, Arthur, 8
Blaisdell, Donald, 9
Brannan Plan, 60
Brookings Institution, 107
Buchanan Committee, 49
Budget and Accounting Act,
36
Bundy, McGeorge, 18
Bureau leaders' influence, 69-
87
choosing committees, 80-1
exploiting hearings, 81-4

interpersonal influence, 78-
80
maintaining liaison, 76-8
using higher support, 70-6
using publicity, 84-7
Bureau of the Budget, 36-7,
52
Bureau of Indian Affairs, 44-5,
54, 68, 71-2, 74-5, 77,
79-80, 86-7, 90-5, 97-8,
100, 102, 114-15, 117-18
Bureau of Reclamation, 45
Bureaucratic propaganda, 74,
84-7
Burke, Charles H., 79
Burns, James M., 17

Cannon, Joe, 26
Cater, Douglass, 6, 25, 68
Checks and balances, 14-15
Clientele groups, 88-91
Cohen, Felix, 77
Collier, John, 44, 71-5, 79-81,
86-7, 90, 102, 108, 110,
118
Commissioner of Indian Af-
fairs, role and office, 37,
75-6, 80, 92-3, 95
Committee influence upon ad-
ministration of laws, 96-7
Committee staff influence,
111-12

Committees on Indian Affairs
general, 44, 53-4, 80, 93,
110, 114-15, 117-18
House, 74, 79, 81, 99-101
Senate, 45, 74, 79, 81, 98-
101, 108-9
Investigating subcommittees,
House, 109
Senate, 107-9
Congress, committee roles, 54-
5
Senate-House contrasts, 47-
8
structure, 46
Congressional decentralization,
24-7, 55
influence on subsystem, 46-
55, 64
influence via reorganization,
48-50
limitations on control, 50-4
Coolidge Administration, 79,
118
Cooptation, 94-6
Corps of Engineers, 45
Cosmopolitan groups, 92-3
Council of Economic Advisors,
51
Cyclical patterns of group ef-
fects, 115-18, 129

Dewey, Thomas E., 61
Dies Committee, 109-11
Dillon, C. Douglas, 18
Durkin, Martin, 19

Eisenhower Administration, 23
Eisenhower, Dwight, 18, 40
Employee interests, 88-91
Escalation of issues, 22, 61

FBI, 37

Factors in committee response,
112-15
Farm Bureau, 56, 58, 60-1
Farmers Union, 56, 58
Federal government growth, 3-
5
Feedback, 69-70

General setting, defined, 11
Gillette, Guy, 51
Glavis, Louis, 107
Goldwater, Barry, 57
Gompers, Samuel, 56
Grass-roots groups, 92-4
Griffith, Ernest S., 6
Group consultation, 94-6

Harding Administration, 118
Harris, Joseph P., 9, 97
Herring, Pendleton, 8
Hitler, Adolph, 94
Hobby, Oveta Culp, 18
Hoover Administration, 45,
106-7
Hoover, J. Edgar, 37
Hope, Clifford R., 60
Hope-Aiken Law, 60-1
Howard, Edward, 79
Humphrey, Hubert H., 60-1
Huzar, Elias, 52
Hyneman, Charles, 97

Ickes, Anna Willmarth, 72
Ickes, Harold L., 18, 44, 71-2,
74-5, 90, 102, 110
Indian Reorganization Act, 72-
4, 98-9
Institutionalizing personal relations, 80, 95
Interior Department, 77, 107
Investigating committee influence, 103-6
committee types, 106-11

Jefferson, Thomas, 40
Johnson, Jed, 102
Johnson, Lyndon B., 18, 26, 41
Joint Committee on Atomic Energy, 52
    on Economic Report, 53

Keefe, William J., 97
Kefauver Committee, 105, 107
Kennedy, John F., 18
Key, V. O., Jr., 3, 8
Kline, Allan B., 60-1

LaFollette-Monroney Act, 24, 48-50
Latham, Earl, 10
Legal norms, 14-15
Legislative Reference Service, 49
Leiserson, Avery, 8
Lodge, Henry Cabot, 18

Maass, Arthur, 45
McCarthy Committee, 51, 78, 105, 107
McCarthy, Joseph, 40, 51, 78
McClellan Committee, 105, 107
McNamara, Robert S., 18
Milbrath, Lester, 9
Mundt, Karl, 81, 109

NAACP, 57
Neo-conservatism, 33
Neustadt, Richard, 33-4
Non-internal interest groups, 91-4
Norms for bureaucrats in committee hearings, 82-3

Ogul, Morris S., 97

Parties, coalitions, 17-20
    decentralization, 27-8
    factions, 16-17, 19-20
    functions, 16
Partisan and non-partisan issues, 21-2
Party government, 15-22
Party influence, general, 55-62, 64-5
    and groups, 55-9
    conditions favoring, 59-62
Pluralism, 4, 5
Policy-making, defined, 12
    system, 15-23
Presidency, expansion of, 33-5
Presidential influence, 14, 23, 24, 33-46, 62-4
    assessment of, 43-6
    hierarchical, 35-40
    informal, 40-2
    limitations, 42-3

Riggs, Fred, 10
Role conflicts, 79-80
Roosevelt, Franklin D., 18, 44-5, 71-2, 75, 106
Rules Committee, House, 26, 47
Rules Committee, Senate, 51

Saxon, James J., 41
Selznick, Philip, 94
Semi-autonomy in political system, 22-8, 31
    of bureaus, 23-4
    of committees, 24-7
    of groups, 27-8
Seniority, 29-30
Separation of powers, 14-15
Staff liaison, 77-8
Strategic sensitivity, 69
Strategy and influence, 69-87
"Sub-governments," 6

Substantive committee influence, 98-101
memberships, 100-1
Subsystem leaders, 28-30
Subsystems, general, 4-8, 11
propositions about, 121-9
relations with general system, 32-65
relations within, 66-118
summarized, 119-20

Taft, Robert, 19
Thomas, Elmer, 73, 98, 109
Truman, David, 8
Truman, Harry S, 40

Truman Administration, 106

Veterans Administration, 89

Wallas, Graham, 8
Werner, Theodore B., 115
Wheeler, Burton K., 45, 98, 107
"Whirlpools" of government, 6
Wilson, Woodrow, 9, 26, 33, 34
Woll, Peter, 97

Zeigler, Harmon, 9